The Baltimore Elite Giants

BOB LUKE

The Baltimore Elite Giants

*Sport and Society in the
Age of Negro League Baseball*

THE JOHNS HOPKINS UNIVERSITY PRESS
BALTIMORE

The Johns Hopkins University Press
2715 North Charles Street
Baltimore, Maryland 21218-4363
www.press.jhu.edu

Library of Congress Cataloging-in-Publication Data
Luke, Bob.
The Baltimore Elite Giants : sport and society in the age of
Negro league baseball / Bob Luke.
    p. cm.
Includes bibliographical references and index.
ISBN-13: 978-0-8018-9116-8 (hardcover : alk. paper)
ISBN-10: 0-8018-9116-7 (hardcover : alk. paper)
1. Baltimore Elite Giants (baseball team)—History. 2. Negro
leagues—History. 3. African American baseball players—
History. 4. Discrimination in sports—United States—History.
5. Baseball—Maryland—Baltimore—History. I. Title.
GV875.N35L85 2009
796.357'64097526—dc22   2008028735

A catalog record for this book is available from the British Library.

Illustration credits may be found on the last printed page of
this book.

*Special discounts are available for bulk puchases of this book. For
more information, please contact Special Sales at 410-516-6936 or
specialsales@press.jhu.edu.*

The Johns Hopkins University Press uses environmentally friendly
book materials, including recycled text paper that is composed of
at least 30 percent post-consumer waste, whenever possible. All
of our book papers are acid-free, and our jackets and covers are
printed on paper with recycled content.

For Judy

CONTENTS

The Baltimore Elite Giants

PROLOGUE

Baseball on a Shoestring

The five-game series between the Baltimore Elite (pro-nounced e-e-e-light) Giants and the Washington-Home-stead Grays to determine the Negro National League championship for 1948 was one of the strangest series of games in all of professional baseball. At the end of the eighth inning of the third game, played Friday night, September 17th at Bugle Field in East Baltimore, the teams were tied 4–4. The inning ended at 10:52 p.m., just before the city's 11:15 p.m. curfew. Grays manager Vic Harris and umpire Mo Har-ris, an ex-Gray and brother of Vic,[1] told the white umpire-in-chief, Ted Lewis, there was not enough time to complete the ninth inning. Lewis disagreed and ordered the Grays to bat. Thanks to two walks and four consecutive hits, the Grays scored three runs and loaded the bases.

The Elites had lost the two previous games, 6–0 and 5–3. Fearing they would lose this game and the pennant if the ninth inning were com-pleted, the Elites refused to make outs, hoping to extend play beyond 11:15. "I threw the ball to right field instead of throwing to first base and let 'em run," Frazier Robinson, the Elites catcher, said. "We let 'em run all the runs they wanted to run just so we could prolong the inning."[2] The Elites believed that if play continued beyond 11:15 and the game was called, the score would revert to what it was at the end of the eighth inning, 4–4. A tie game would not count in the series. Lewis called the game at 11:15. The Elites thought they had new life.

Negro National League president Rev. John H. Johnson thought oth-

1

erwise. He telephoned Elites owner Vernon Green and Vic Harris on Sunday, just minutes before the fourth game was to start, and ordered the teams to continue Friday night's game from the point where it had been called. Green refused. He said it would be unfair to charge fans to see the end of a playoff game and not an entire playoff game as they were expecting. If the teams completed Friday's game first and the Grays held their lead, which they most likely would, thereby taking the series, Bugle Field patrons would be reduced to sitting through an exhibition game. Green told Johnson, "Standing on my rights as a club owner and one sworn to protect the Baltimore fans as best I can, I don't intend to abide by this order until a more thorough investigation is made by your office."[3] Johnson agreed to come to Baltimore on Monday to talk things over.

Meanwhile, the Elites and Grays played the scheduled Sunday game. Spitballer Bill Byrd threw a five-hitter at the Grays while Lester Lockett and Johnny Washington contributed four and five RBIs respectively to lead the Elites to an 11–3 win and keep them alive, so they believed, in the playoffs.[4] Following the last out of the fourth game, three Grays players ran from their dugout and took up positions on the bases. Green ordered his players to the locker room and told them to change into street clothes. After several minutes, the Grays sat down on the bases. After several more minutes, Vic Harris motioned them back to the dugout. Harris, somehow thinking Friday's game was to be completed at the end of the Sunday game, had ordered the three Grays runners to take their bases.

After meeting with the umpires on Monday, Johnson ruled that the chief umpire had erred in his instructions to the teams on Friday night. League rules, Johnson said, stated that no inning should start after 11:00 p.m. but that any inning starting before 11:00 had to be completed. Lewis should have told the teams that the ninth inning would be completed even if play went beyond 11:15. His failure to do so contributed to the Elites' stalling, which Johnson ruled was unsportsmanlike and therefore grounds for the game to be forfeited to the Grays, 9–0. His decision gave the pennant to the Grays.[5]

A league president's deciding a pennant race because the crew chief

Pitcher Bill "Daddy" Byrd, 1947. He retired in 1950 after compiling a 114–72 record with the Elites.

did not know the rules is given as one glaring example of the challenges Negro leaguers in general, and the Baltimore Elite Giants in particular, faced when compared to their white, major league counterparts. Lacking experienced umpiring crews, like those who traveled with the major league teams throughout the season, Negro league teams often had to contract with umpires, some better than others, each time they arrived in a city.

Another challenge was the way players were found and trained. The "farm system" consisted of a loose association of semipro teams. There were no scouts or position coaches. Players came to the attention of owners through recommendations of other players, by a player asking for a tryout, or when a team official happened to see a man play. An example of the last occurred when Joe Black and Cal Irvin, brother of future Hall of Famer Monte Irvin and a fellow student with Black at Morgan State College (now Morgan State University), were knocking several of the Elites during a game in the spring of 1943. A well-dressed gentleman sit-

Lester Lockett, 1948, outfielder and third baseman for the Elites from 1947 to 1949

ting behind them in the grandstand leaned over and said, "I couldn't help overhearing you fellows talking. Are you really that good?" The gentleman was Vernon Green, then business manager for the Elites. Black had a tryout and proved to be "that good." Cal Irvin turned down a tryout because his parents did not want him to lose his amateur status.[6]

Players improved their craft through trial and error and with occasional coaching from fellow players or the team's player-manager. Harold Gould, right-handed pitcher for the Philadelphia Stars from 1947 to 1948, got his first coaching from an umpire. As Gould told the story: "We didn't realize we had any talent. We'd have a pick-up game and someone said, 'Harold, you want to pitch?' and I said, 'Yeah. I don't know nothin' about pitching, but yeah, I'll pitch.' I was so wild the umpire said, 'You ain't never gonna throw a strike.' The umpire told me, 'You gotta get the ball between the letters and the knees, that's where the ball gotta be.' That was my first lesson in baseball."[7] Some players had written contracts, some did not. Players "jumped" contracts with one team for a contract with another team when they saw more inviting opportunities. Owners raided other teams by offering players more money. Ros-

Johnny Washington, 1948, hard-hitting first baseman for the Elites in 1941 and 1946–48

ters were on the order of fifteen to eighteen players, as opposed to the standard twenty-five-man major league roster, which meant that Negro leaguers played multiple positions. Many pitchers, for instance, played the outfield or pinch hit when not on the mound.

The teams' league schedules varied in the number of games from year to year, and not all teams played the same number of league games in a given year, a situation that caused disputes about where teams finished in the standings. The Elites, like most Negro league teams, never owned a stadium. Instead, they paid booking agents to arrange a game and they paid rent to the stadium owner. The fees and rentals ate away at the teams' revenues.

Financial shortages and the racial attitudes of the day further contributed to the precariousness of the business operations. Many major league owners drew on family fortunes. Boston Red Sox owner Tom Yawkey inherited a family-run, multimillion-dollar iron and lumber business. New York Yankees head Jacob Ruppert's family made millions in the beer business, as did the Busch family, owners of the St. Louis Cardinals. Owners without a family fortune, such as Clark Griffith of the Washington Senators, exercised their business acumen. Often they profited from segregation by renting their stadiums to Negro league teams.

Negro league team owners, including the Elites' founder, Thomas T. "Smiling Tom" Wilson of Nashville, Tennessee, were men of means within the black community. Clinton "Butch" McCord, Nashville native and right fielder for the Elites from 1948 to 1950, described Wilson as a powerful businessman with a generous spirit. "Wilson," McCord said, "was a big shot. He introduced the interurban bus route from Nashville to Franklin with his wife, a doctor named Bertha." According to Mc-Cord, the black community looked upon Wilson as "a bootlegger or a Godfather."[8]

A successful entrepreneur, Wilson built his wealth on activities both legal and illegal. He ran a profitable numbers operation, which was illegal, sponsored numerous events at his namesake stadium in Nashville, Wilson Park, and ran a popular nightclub, the Paradise Ballroom. A 1942 article in the *Chicago Defender* cited Wilson as one of three "leaders in Nashville city life." His community service activities in Nashville included a term as chairman of the board of the Pride of Tennessee Elks Lodge No. 1102.[9]

When asked if people feared Wilson, McCord said, "No, you just respected the man."[10] In much the same vein, Hall of Famer Roy Campanella, who caught for the Elites from 1938 to 1945 and chose to spend a year playing in the Mexican leagues due to a dispute with Wilson, said of him, "He was a tough man at times, but a real fair man too. The nicest and truest thing that I can say about him is that he was a sportsman all the way."[11]

In addition to his business and civic activities, Wilson enjoyed the good life. Luther Carmichael, a Nashville sportswriter, recalled Wilson as a "happy-go-lucky fellow who paid everything in cash." "Wilson," Carmichael added, "liked a good time and was very proper with the ladies." The ladies no doubt appreciated Wilson's being a sharp dresser; he favored custom-made, pin-stripe suits and was always in possession of "a big wad of cash."[12]

Some of Wilson's counterparts, for example Gus Greenlee, owner

An Asset to Baseball

THOMAS T. WILSON
PRESIDENT
NEGRO NATIONAL BASEBALL LEAGUE
OWNER
BALTIMORE ELITE GIANTS

Thomas T. "Smiling Tom" Wilson, 1943, Elites founder and owner, 1921–47

of the Pittsburgh Crawfords, Abe and Effa Manley, co-owners of the Newark Eagles, and James "Soldier Boy" Semler of the New York Black Yankees, also came by their wealth by running numbers, developing real estate, and owning restaurants or clubs. An interesting variation on this pattern was Homestead Grays' owner, Cumberland Posey, a former player, who relied on Rufus "Sonnyman" Jackson for financial support. Jackson derived his wealth from the numbers business, the hundreds of jukeboxes he rented out to area bars and cafes, and a Pittsburgh night-club he owned, the Sky Rocket Café. Posey made the decisions but stayed above the financial fray. He wrote a column for the *Pittsburgh Courier*, served on the Homestead (Pennsylvania) School Board, and enjoyed membership in several elite Pittsburgh clubs.[13] Though wealthy by the standards of black society, these men's resources fell fall short of those of major league owners.

Negro league owners also had to contend with white society's view of them and their business operations, which was that they were shady, seedy, and criminal. The black community, however, looked upon these men as pillars of society and friends one could count on for help. Greenlee, like Wilson, supported civic causes, backing a soup kitchen, bankrolling political candidates, and helping the *Pittsburgh Courier* during hard times.[14]

In spite of the challenges, the Elites played the game as well, and often better, than did their white counterparts. The Elites won the majority of the postseason games against the crosstown Orioles, of the International League. The Elites brought two league championships to Baltimore (1939 and 1949) and one Negro League World Series championship (1949). When not winning the pennant, they were usually in hot pursuit of it, frequently battling the Washington-Homestead Grays down to the last one or two games of the season. By 1942 the Elites-Grays games had achieved rivalry status. Fans from both cities flocked to the games.[15] The Grays built a dynasty by winning eight Negro National League pennants between 1937 and 1945 (or nine depending on how you count the outcome of the 1939 race). Hall of Famers Josh Gibson (the "black Babe Ruth"), Walter "Buck" Leonard (the "black Lou Gehrig"), James "Cool Papa" Bell, Ray Brown, and Jud Wilson starred for the Grays, as did Vic Harris and Sam Bankhead. The Elites featured Hall of Famers Biz Mackey and Roy Campanella and future Brooklyn Dodger stalwarts Joe Black and Junior Gilliam.

During the Elites' stay in the Monumental City, from 1938 to 1951, black professionals in other fields in Baltimore, like those in baseball uniforms, also performed outstandingly. Black lawyers, doctors, writers, teachers, musicians, shopkeepers, pipe fitters, and steelworkers counted among their numbers individuals whose skills were as good as or better than those of some whites in the same lines of work. Yet Jim Crow laws and discriminatory customs kept the races separated, according blacks

Elites catchers Robert Clarke (left) *and Roy Campanella* (right) *discuss strategy at Bugle Field in 1942*

second-class treatment. Black children made up one-third of the city's public school population in 1938, but they attended classes in buildings that were unsanitary, overcrowded, and, in many cases, had been condemned. Their parents had no voice on the all-white school board.

Bad feelings and occasional violence occurred between blacks and whites in Baltimore. In December 1938, on Pennsylvania Avenue, three white Northwestern District police officers beat Joseph Dunlap, a black man, to the point that he almost lost his sight. Eyewitnesses signed affidavits declaring that the altercation was unprovoked. The Communist Party urged Police Commissioner Robert Stanton to suspend and prosecute the officers involved, Leo Williams, George Tapkin, and Charles Field, and to issue a public assurance that he would stop all police brutal-

Joe Black following through after delivering his fastball, 1947

ity in the city. Instead, Judge Eli Frank, sitting on the Supreme Bench of Baltimore City, found Dunlap guilty of disorderly conduct and fined him one cent.[17] Several months later, police killed four young black men under questionable circumstances. Despite repeated attempts by lawyers of the National Association for the Advancement of Colored People (NAACP) to prosecute the officers, Judge John H. Stanford, a police justice in the Northwestern District, refused to bring the officers before a grand jury.[18]

Interracial marriage was illegal. In the fall of 1938 police arrested Willoughby Wilson, a black man, and Mabel Showacre, who was white, for marrying and put them in jail in Annapolis, the state capital. A judge dropped the charges against Showacre and released Wilson on a suspended sentence.[19] Greyhound bus drivers could deny blacks permission to board buses and remove those who refused to sit in the back.[20] White businesses posted "Whites Only" signs (also "Gentiles Only" signs). Most theaters had separate sections for whites and blacks. Restaurants served either blacks or whites but not both. The faculty club at Johns Hopkins University at first denied admittance to a newly hired black faculty member.[21] The Maryland Institute's School of Fine and Practical Arts told a black applicant in 1943, "We do not accept colored students."[22]

Aviation manufacturing corporation Glenn L. Martin's stance toward hiring blacks at this time was typical of the discrimination that many Baltimore industries practiced. In 1941, Martin personnel manager D. W. Siemon said, "The firm has no intention of 'pioneering' in the field of defense jobs for colored people . . . We know that white workers may not work well with colored men. If the government would take the lead . . . industry could feel free to follow its example."[23] Three months later, on June 25, 1941, Franklin Roosevelt did just that when he issued Executive Order 8802, prohibiting such discrimination. The order charged a committee in the Office of Production Management to investigate complaints of discrimination and "take appropriate steps to redress grievances which it finds to be valid."[24] Roosevelt's order supported the efforts of groups seeking equal treatment for blacks in Baltimore, including the Congress of Industrial Organizations (CIO) and the NAACP.

Many blacks had to live in subpar housing, a situation caused by slum clearance projects, inattentive landlords, the large numbers of blacks who streamed into the city in search of work in Baltimore's dozens of war industries as World War II got under way, and housing covenants (clauses in deeds prohibiting the sale of a house to people of ethnic or racial minorities, e.g., blacks, Jews, and Syrians). Seventy percent of the housing designated for African Americans in Baltimore was declared substandard in 1945.[25]

The Negro league ball games offered blacks a sanctuary where they could get away from such treatment for a couple of hours. In the words of Stanley Glenn, a catcher for the Philadelphia Stars 1944–50,

Negro league baseball was a great happening. The ballpark was one place you could vent. There were so few places to go. Only black-owned restaurants could you go to. Philadelphia, Baltimore, it didn't matter. Black folk had so little to do that they went to the ballpark. It was the number-one place to go after church. And we had open seating. At least 20 percent of the fans were white. They sat anywhere. We never had that crap. Ladies came dressed in their Sunday best—high-heeled shoes, silk stockings, long-sleeved gloves, and hats on their heads. They'd sit there in the 90-degree heat. Men came in their Sunday suits complete with tie, hat, and shined shoes.[26]

The players also dressed well, but not always out of choice. Wilson allowed no jeans, even on the team bus. He wanted his players, when they stepped off the bus on Sundays, to look as if they were going to church. Wilson expected his players to be well mannered and avoid profanity. "Before we'd even take on a player," Wilson said, "we'd want to know something about his character. If we got the word he was a heavy drinker or something we wouldn't have him."[27]

Fans did not let their wardrobe prevent them from having a rollicking good time, according to one who, on many a Sunday, watched the Grays perform against the Elites and other teams at Griffith Stadium, in the heart of Washington's black community, at the intersection of Florida Avenue and Seventh Street, N.W. (The Howard University Medical

Three African American aircraft workers assembling the pilot's compartment of a bomber plane at the Glenn L. Martin Company's segregated plant on Oldham Street in the Canton section of Baltimore, 1942. Following President Roosevelt's executive order, the company hired blacks, but it maintained a segregated work force.

School occupies the site today.) The fan told sportswriter Prentice Mills, "I remember Cool Papa Bell and Josh Gibson. I remember Satchel Paige. I remember the concession barkers and their jokes and banter. There was an atmosphere of excitement, like at a circus. People were buying programs and pennants. They were buying hot dogs and peanuts and screaming and yelling."[28] Ronald Crockett, who also attended Grays games at Griffith Stadium, remembered fans who "camped out in the stadium with picnic lunches, fried chicken, and, sometimes, illicit bottles of whiskey." Frank Sullivan, who worked at the Library of Congress, remembered riding the trolley for a dime from his home near the Navy Yard in southeast D.C. across town to Griffith Stadium. "It was," Sullivan said, "like the Ringling Brothers' Circus." Sullivan recalled a triple play by the Grays after which "the crowd went wild for what seemed like 15 minutes. After the game," he continued, "people ran on the field to shake hands with the players, and they'd sign autographs . . . The atmosphere inside Griffith Stadium was like a rock concert."[29]

Players and fans mingled after games. Glenn said of the women in the stands, "If you were a decent kind of guy, some of them wanted you to meet their family and would invite you over for dinner. They were a bunch of fine girls. Some of us married those girls. We had places we'd go after games. Philly and Baltimore had all kind of honky-tonk places where the bands would go, like Basie and Ellington, and all the big bands of that era. We'd hear the bands, and dance and have a drink or two. You're riding the transit system down and back and everybody knows who you are so nothing's going to happen to you."[30]

This book examines how segregation and discrimination affected the Elites operation—finding a ballpark, surviving financially, offering a sanctuary to the city's black community. It draws on articles from the black newspapers of the time; interviews with Baltimore residents and former players; documents from the Baltimore City Archives; the papers of Branch Rickey, Jackie Robinson, Theodore McKeldin, and the NAACP; private photograph collections; the Newark Eagles' office records on file at the Newark (New Jersey) Public Library, among other documents and publications. The reader will find summaries of each season and descriptions of key games that highlight the team's fortunes and the performances of players whose names often are now known only to baseball historians. The book also discusses how the integration of organized baseball affected white Baltimoreans. An epilogue captures the ironic and bittersweet outcomes that integration visited on the Elites and on Baltimore. Appendices supply a brief history of black baseball in Baltimore; display a breakdown of the team's revenue and expenses for 1947, the only year for which such information has been found; and show where the Elites finished in the standings each year they were in Baltimore.

High Hopes

Receptive Community

Newspapers often referred to Smiling Tom Wilson's squad as "the well-traveled Elite Giants." They played their first game in 1921 in Nashville, Tennessee, and joined the Negro National League in 1929. The Great Depression caused the league to disband in 1932. The Elites rejoined the league when it reappeared in 1933. When he discovered that the East Coast teams found getting to and from Nashville a financial hardship, Wilson moved the franchise to Detroit, and they started the 1935 season there. But the Elites left Detroit after several weeks—they could not find a stadium to rent—and went to Columbus, Ohio, for the rest of the '35 season. There the city's modest black population (32,774 in 1930) could not muster sufficient support for the team,[1] so Wilson again pulled up stakes, moving the Elites to Washington, D.C., for the 1936 and '37 seasons. In May 1938 he moved the team to Baltimore, where he at last found adequate community support.

Between 1920 and 1930, as blacks arrived from low-income rural areas in Virginia, North Carolina, and South Carolina, Baltimore's black population increased five times faster than that of whites. The trend continued while the Elites were in town. From 1930 to 1950 the number of African Americans in the city grew from 142,000 (21% of the total city

Tom Wilson's 1927 Nashville Elite Giants at Athletic Park, Nashville, Tennessee

population) to 225,000 (31%).[2] Most blacks lived in a horseshoe pattern around the center city, the open side of the horseshoe facing north.[3]

The majority of poor and working-class blacks lived in East Baltimore, the site of the Elites' home park, Bugle Field. Many were on Public Assistance. Working-class blacks also congregated in areas of South Baltimore, the site of Maryland Park, which had been home to the Baltimore Black Sox and where the Elites' last venue, Westport Ball Park, was built. Fortunately for Wilson, Baltimore also had a sizeable black middle class, most of whom lived in Old West. This "city within a city"[4] was bounded to the north and south by North Avenue and Franklin Street and to the east and west by Druid Hill and Fulton Avenues.[5] Although best known for its upper-middle-class, professional, black neighborhoods, Old West also had pockets of slum housing. Of the 166,000 blacks living in Baltimore in 1940,[6] 125,000 lived in Old West, which, a resident later recalled, "was a tightly knit community where you knew almost everyone and had access to the best black teachers and doctors."[7] By 1933, twenty-five of the city's thirty-eight black physicians, fifteen dentists, and seventeen pharmacists lived and worked in Old West. Many had graduated from the city's only black high school, Frederick Douglass High School. The school's faculty included one member with a doctorate, six with masters degrees, three Harvard graduates, three from Fisk, fourteen from Howard, three from Brown University, and one from the University of Pennsylvania.[8] Children from most of Old West's middle-class black families attended Douglass, including Thurgood Marshall, the nation's first black Supreme Court justice, whose uncle, Cyrus Marshall, taught algebra;[9] entertainer Cab Calloway; civil rights leader Clarence Mitchell Jr. and his wife, Juanita Jackson, also a civil rights force in the country; and Victorine Adams, the wife of black Baltimore's richest man, William "Little Willie" L. Adams, and the first black woman to sit on the Baltimore City Council.[10]

Entrepreneurs in Old West included real estate salesmen, photographers, house painters, and grocers. Ernest Perkins is offered as an example of an entrepreneurial grocer. Perkins established his grocery store at the intersection of Lanvale and Calhoun Streets in 1934, following graduation from Lincoln University and a job as a field agent with the Colored Merchant Association of New York City. He joined Baltimore's previously all-white Independent Retailers Association and applied the association's principles in founding the Colored Grocery Association of Baltimore. The value of Perkins's business increased fivefold over three years, even though he had "plenty of white competition at the corners and within the blocks of his neighborhood." He explained his success by saying that he gave people, including whites, "what they want, when they want it, and how they want it."[11] The Druid Hill Laundry at 1634 Druid Hill Avenue, established in 1896, was another success story. By 1938 it was grossing $40,000 a year.[12]

Some entrepreneurs, such as Clarence "Shad" Brown, pursued both legal and illegal activities. Brown opened Shad Brown's Bail Bonds on Pennsylvania Avenue in the late 1930s and achieved a reputation as "an icon of entrepreneurial success by adding a travel agency that sponsored tours to Atlantic City in the pre-casino days and expanded his business to include tours to other locations in the United States, Canada, Europe,

Photograph of an architectural sketch showing the southwest façade of the old Frederick Douglass High School at North Calhoun and Baker Streets in Baltimore

Bahamas, and Bermuda."[13] Brown also had a business relationship with city judges.

Judges running for office would come to me to introduce them to Willie Adams. They came to us to get votes. When they got elected, they offered to give me money. I said, "I got money. I want favors." Say you got locked up for beating somebody. If you got six months or a year, I'd walk up to you and give you my card and say I might get you a favor. Then I'd go see the judge who would say to me, "See if you can get $500 from the family. We'll split it down." I'd go back and tell the judge that your family didn't have but $300 and we'd split it down, $150 each. But your family had really given me $500. Everybody had their trick. Then the judge would suspend your sentence or give you less time. Judges were only getting $5,000 a year. Why would they pay a lot of money to run? They knew what they were doing. They'd make money.[14]

Enterprising teenagers made money in Old West, among them jazz singer and bandleader Cab Calloway, who grew up in Old West. He sold copies of the *Baltimore Sun* for three cents a copy to people who passed through Old West on streetcars on their way to work in downtown Baltimore. "I'd ride all the way up to Madison Avenue," Calloway said, "to the car barn on one car, then I'd hop a car coming downtown and sell the papers all the way back."[15] Frederick Lonesome, who grew up in Old West in the 600 block of West Lanvale as one of eleven children, was another of Old West's teenaged businessmen. Lonesome remembered "doing every kind of job you could think of—selling papers, working on vegetable trucks, writing numbers. I'd walk through black neighborhoods looking for work. I wouldn't go through the white neighborhoods deliberately, but sometimes I'd have to cut through them. I could run pretty good." Lonesome remembers the Jewish neighborhoods as being more friendly. "They wouldn't bother you. Jewish people owned a lot of places and got a lot of black people jobs. They treated you much better than the rednecks—that's what we used to call 'em."[16]

Among the prominent black families in Old West were the Murphys, whose newspaper, the *Baltimore Afro-American*, gained national prominence. With a circulation of 200,000, it served as the primary source of information about the Elites' fortunes. The Carters ran a catering business. The Smiths imported goods from the world over. The Wilson family (no relation to Tom) made insurance available to Old West residents. The Coleman family ran a large publishing company.

These and other families owned large houses on wide streets. W. E. B. DuBois, civil rights pioneer and noted sociologist and historian, referred to neighborhoods like Old West as "showpieces of contemporary Black America."[17] Families of all social strata in Old West took family life seriously. Extended family networks welcomed the cousin who arrived from North Carolina and helped him or her get established. Word of a birth, death, marriage, divorce, promotion, or job loss spread quickly. Parents enforced their children's bedtimes, expected them to arrive home from school at a certain time, took active roles in parent-teacher associations, and fed them three hearty meals a day.[18]

Old West residents had a long history of political activism. A clergymen's association, the Ministerial Alliance, led a march to Annapolis in 1902 to protest segregated railways and steamships. Baltimore's chapter of the NAACP, the nation's second oldest, had its headquarters in Old West near Thurgood Marshall's home. The Young People's Forum, a precursor to the NAACP and staffed by younger members of the prominent black families, opened its doors in 1931 in Old West. The Forum led boycotts and formed picket lines to protest establishments on Pennsylvania Avenue, the main street in Old West, that would not serve Negroes.

Their efforts, known by the slogan "Don't Shop Where You Can't Work," first bore fruit in 1934 when the local A&P grocery store hired its first black employee.[19]

Churches such as Sharp Street Methodist, Madison Street Presbyterian, Union Baptist, and Bethel A.M.E. played a central role in the life of Old West by offering citizens more than a place of worship. Bethel hosted speakers who included Olympic champion Jesse Owens, diplomat Ralph Bunche, and birth control advocate Margaret Sanger. On August 25, 1943, Bethel hosted the forty-third annual conference of the National Negro Business League and Housewives League. Twenty-five hundred people crammed into the church to hear Treasury Secretary Henry Morganthau Jr., Maryland governor Herbert O'Conor, Maryland U.S. senator George L. Radcliffe, Mayor Theodore R. McKeldin, and others praise the Negro contribution to the war effort.[20] Newly elected Republican mayor McKeldin told the crowd, "I am proud to be one of those to record the fact that men and women of the great Negro race . . . are in the production of ships and planes . . . in the foxholes . . . fighting, suffering, dying that the glorious heritage of liberty bestowed upon their race by Abraham Lincoln shall be preserved in this generation for them and for all of us."[21]

Churches also served as concert halls. Roland Hayes, an internationally known tenor, came out of retirement to perform for a capacity crowd at the Sharp Street church in this segregated era when white theaters such as the Lyric were closed to blacks. The *Afro-American* reported that Hayes "held his audience spellbound with his rendition of popular spirituals through which he has thrilled even royalty."[22]

Pennsylvania Avenue was the "social Mecca" for Old West. There blacks had their choice of cafés—Eddie's Café, Woolf's Café, the Dreamland Café, Inc., the Alhambra Grill, advertising itself as "Baltimore's Finest," at 1520 Pennsylvania Avenue—as well as clubs that carried names like Sphinx, Frolic Café and Lounge, Ubangi, and Moonglow. However, those who imbibed too much could find themselves spending the night locked "under the clock," a lofty clock adorning the Northwestern Police Station.[23] A game of pool could be played at several Pennsylvania Avenue pool halls, including the Belmont Billiard Parlor and the Royal Pool

Parlor.[24] Women went to the Charm Center, owned by Victorine Adams, for top-of-the-line New York fashion. There they tried on clothes, which they were not allowed to do in Baltimore's downtown stores.[25] Men took their wives or girlfriends to the Green Room Restaurant in the York Hotel, a block off "The Avenue," at 1200 Madison Avenue for fine dining. They indulged in soul food at Mrs. Clarke's Boarding House, a block south of York, at 1100 Madison Avenue. Jazz artists Dinah Washington and Nat King Cole held forth at the Casino Club, owned by Willie Adams,[26] or at the Royal Theater. Whites wishing to hear these artists came to "The Strip," as Pennsylvania Avenue was also known, because black musicians could not play downtown. The same Jim Crow policies that kept Negro leaguers out of the majors kept black musicians out of Baltimore's downtown hotels. Clarence Brown remembered Dinah Washington staying at his house because she "couldn't just go downtown and get one of those hotels down there. No, if you were black you had to stay at someone's house on the Avenue if the nice hotels that served Negroes [the Penn or the York] were booked."[27] Brown added, "Dinah Washington, Pearl Bailey, Count Basie, and Earl Hines could only stay on Pennsylvania Avenue, and they paid $5.00 a night to stay at a colored man's house."[28]

Frederick Lonesome enjoyed the social life along Pennsylvania Avenue: "On Saturday night, I'd make sure I had my best clothes on and I'd get on the Avenue. I'd walk north all the way up to the North Avenue, where the Met [white-owned Metropolitan movie theater] was; that was the end of the black territory, and then I'd walk back down on the other side of the street." The Royal Theater, which featured big bands and jazz combos, was Lonesome's favorite place. "That was really great for me. You had the whites, like Tommy Dorsey, Benny Goodman, and Charlie Barnet. And of course Duke Ellington, Count Basie, Cab Calloway, and Louis Armstrong."[29] Originally built as the Douglass Theater by the black-owned Douglass Amusement Company, the Royal dominated the 1300 block of Pennsylvania Avenue.[30] In later years, Lonesome missed the trolley rides on Pennsylvania Avenue the most. "We could ride the cars all night on Saturday night. It was nice and cool on those hot nights."[31]

The Regent Theater, 1941, a vaudeville and movie house at 1629 Pennsylvania Avenue, could seat 2,000 patrons.

Baltimore, with its large and growing black population and large black middle class, was just the kind of city Wilson needed for his baseball team.

Settling In

Tom Wilson's first challenge was to get Baltimore's black community behind the team. Richard D. Powell led the campaign. Born in Silver Spring, Maryland, in 1912, Powell and his family later moved to Baltimore, where, as a teenager, he followed the Baltimore Black Sox. Powell left school in the eighth grade, when his father died, to help support the family. He worked for bookies, as a fight judge, and as a courier for the federal government, meeting many people in the process.[32] Once he heard Wilson was considering a move to Baltimore, Powell set about talking up the team to black leaders and community organizations in Old West, including the Frontiers Club.[33] The club was the Baltimore chapter of the Frontiers Club of America whose purpose was to support minority-group leaders working toward the solution of racial, social, and civic issues. Members included "leading businessmen and civic minded citizens in strategic positions."[34] The club met often at the York Hotel, which Wilson chose as the site of the team's headquarters. Vernon Green, future team owner, and his wife, Henryene, lived at the York during the baseball season, "usually in Room 11, with their dog, hotel furniture, and a large metal filing cabinet," from about 1938 to 1945, according to Green's brother Reginald.[35] Large in stature, Green was known as "Fat Pappy." His association with the Elites started in 1924, when his play as a catcher for a local Nashville nine attracted Wilson's attention. Green's playing career was short-lived, and in 1926 he became the team's bus driver. Wilson promoted him to business manager in 1940.[36]

Powell gained the support of *Afro-American* sports editor Leon Hardwick, who promised to carry articles about the team, many of which Powell himself would write on a second-hand typewriter.[37] Powell gave Negro league players who came through Baltimore in 1937, including members of the Washington Elite Giants, who played some of their 1936 and 1937 games at Bugle Field, a positive view of Baltimore by arranging for some to board in private homes in Old West, where they enjoyed home-cooked meals.[38] Other players stayed at the Clarke Boarding House and ate at segregated restaurants.

By February 1938, Powell's efforts and the good attendance at games the Washington Elites had played in Baltimore in 1936 and 1937 convinced Wilson to move the team forty miles north. Wilson said at the time, "It's been a long time since Baltimore had a regular league team and I feel the people there need one and will support one."[39]

Richard Powell stayed involved with the Elites. He invited players to his home at 1102 Etting Street in Old West for talk and meals and

Richard Powell in his office. Powell held several administrative positions over the Elites' time in Baltimore.

took pitcher Jonas Gaines in as a boarder. Barbara Powell Golden, his daughter, said, "Our house was like the headquarters for the Elites."[40] He hired Jim Handy and John Jefferson to post placards advertising the games up and down Pennsylvania Avenue, as the two men did when Duke Ellington and Count Basie brought their bands to town. "We did real well that way," Powell said. "For a few years we were a better draw than the old International League Orioles."[41]

With support efforts for the team resting in Powell's capable hands, Wilson turned his attention to another pressing matter, finding a ballpark, a process made difficult by a combination of limited funds and racial discrimination. Building one was not an option. He had spent

$75,000 in 1930 to build Wilson Park in Nashville and did not want to repeat the outlay.[42] Baltimore presented Wilson with two ballparks. The first was the 15,000-seat Oriole Park in Waverly, a white neighborhood near the intersection of Greenmount Avenue and 31st Street served by the Number 8 trolley line; it was home to the minor league Baltimore Orioles. The second park was 6,000-seat Bugle Field in a black community in East Baltimore, at the intersection of Edison Highway and Federal Street just beyond the terminus of the Number 27 "trackless trolley" transit line. Trackless trolleys were buses powered by electricity from overhead lines. Wilson preferred the larger Oriole Park, for obvious reasons, but it presented two problems, a long tradition of its owners' not permitting black teams to play there and the necessity of going through a booking agent if the owners could be convinced to rent it to a black team. Booking agents negotiated dates and terms of rent with the white stadium owners and scheduled Negro league teams into stadiums much as they booked circus acts and boxing matches. While arrangements varied, it was not uncommon for teams to pay the stadium owner $1,000 or 25 percent of the gate, whichever was more, for one day or night of baseball. The booking agents would take another 10–15 percent, leaving the two teams to split the remainder of the gate.[43]

Wilson turned reluctantly to two booking agents, Eddie Gottlieb, a white sports entrepreneur based in Philadelphia, and his partner in Baltimore, a black entrepreneur named Douglass O. Smith, to schedule the Elites' games in both Washington and Baltimore.[44] Wilson wanted to contract independently with the stadium owners, but Gottlieb and Smith were able to prevent independent booking.[45]

While Gottlieb is best known for owning and managing professional basketball teams, such as the Philadelphia SPHAs (South Philadelphia Hebrew Association) and the Philadelphia Warriors, his baseball ventures, in addition to booking Negro league games, included an ownership role with the Negro league's Philadelphia Stars. Columnist Red Smith described Gottlieb as "a wonderful little guy about the size and shape of about a half-keg of beer." Gottlieb was enshrined in the Basketball Hall of Fame in 1972.[46] The Eddie Gottlieb trophy is awarded to the National Basketball Association's Rookie of the Year.[47]

Gottlieb and Smith surprised many people when they booked the first Negro league game ever played at Oriole Park, a contest between the Elites and the Pittsburgh Crawfords on May 16, 1937.[48] The press credited the two with "breaking down a racial barrier that had stood for years." Former Oriole Park owners Jack Dunn and Charles Knapp had refused all requests for Negro league teams to play there. The two booking agents also scheduled two Negro league games in Oriole Park later in the year; the 1937 Negro National League champion Homestead Grays and the Chicago American Giants–Kansas City Monarchs All-Star Club, composed mostly of players from those two Negro American League teams, met in Oriole Park on September 26, 1937, for two games of the 1937 Negro League World Series. The players on display included future Hall of Famers Josh Gibson, Willie Wells, "Bullet" Joe Rogan, Willie Foster, and "Turkey" Stearns.[49] Fans were treated to a show of offensive power including a 425-foot smash by Josh Gibson "that landed on a housetop across the alley from the field."[50]

Encouraged by the turnout for the three games, Gottlieb and Smith tried unsuccessfully to schedule all of the Elites' 1938 games in Oriole Park, on dates when the O's were out of town. Oriole management, bowing to white residents in Waverly who did not want black teams playing night games in their neighborhood, refused.[51] Gottlieb and Smith were able to book the Elites into Griffith Stadium for a number of their home games, which helped boost attendance for the Baltimore-based team. For the rest of their home games the Elites were left with Bugle Field in 1938.

Bugle Field was built in 1912 by several young, white, male employees of the Sampson and Doeller Company, a maker of labels for cans. Henry Doeller Sr., the company's president, gave the boys $100 to sponsor their team and said, "The rest is up to you." They cleared a cow pasture east of Belair Road just across the (then) city line, near what is now Edison Highway. The owner, Mrs. Carrie Snyder, rented the field to Doeller's employees for $25 a year. They raised $450 to build a 520-seat covered, wooden grandstand by raffling off Morris chairs in Northeast Baltimore, around Gay Street. They named the field the Label Men's Oval. Their semipro team, the Label Men, won the city championship four

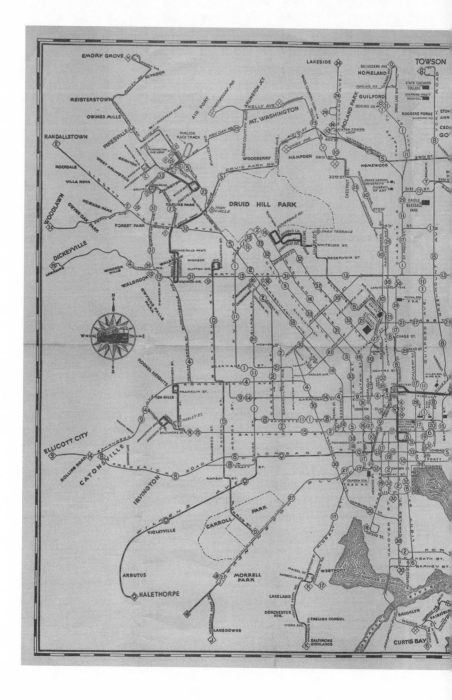

Car, bus, and trackless trolley lines of the Baltimore Transit Company, 1943. Note locations of Oriole Park, south of 31st Street and west of Greenmount Avenue, and Baltimore Stadium (aka Municipal Stadium, the site of Memorial Stadium), on 33rd Street east of Greenmount Avenue. Bugle Field, not shown, was located near the terminus of Street Car Route 27 (middle right, near map title). Westport Ball Park, also not shown, was located near the end of Street Car Line 17, which terminated at Baltimore Highlands (bottom edge of map).

times between 1912 and 1917. Their star pitcher was Eddie Rommel, who later pitched for Connie Mack's Athletics and umpired in the American League. The Label Men sold their lease to the field in 1918, as the war in Europe took many of their players, to Dr. Edward J. Cook. Cook's ball club, St. Andrew's, called the field home until 1924, when Joe Cambria bought the lease for his semipro team, Bugle Coat and Apron. Cambria named the ballpark after his company. Matt Reinhold, whose family lived behind the field, assisted Cambria. The two men later enlarged the field and added bleachers along the first and third base lines. When not in use for baseball, the field hosted amateur and professional soccer games, high school and professional football games, rodeos, lacrosse games, and boxing matches.[52]

Bugle Field was best known for baseball, particularly the Elites' games. Frederick Lonesome would travel from Old West for the games. "It was fun to go see them," he remembered. "You didn't have to have a lot of money to enjoy yourself and you didn't have to be afraid. Once they'd sewn the game up, they'd clown a lot and that was funny. They'd put big hats on, jump up and down, and do all this fancy hitting. The pitchers gave you this big windup like an old Ferris Wheel." "The best games were on Sunday," said Clarence Brown. "It was always a nice time. If you didn't go to the games, you weren't nobody. I always sat right at the front seat because I was very well known. I was a big politician and went to Carter's inauguration."[53]

Brown continued, "If you wanted something stronger than soda or beer, you could buy home-brewed whiskey for $3.00 a pint or $1.50 for a half pint. You'd look for a guy with a long coat on with these bottles sticking all out. The light was gin and the dark was rye. We'd have a good time."[54] Beer could be purchased for 20 cents, a pack of cigarettes for 15 cents, and a soda, bag of peanuts, hot dog, candy, or ice cream could be had for 10 cents.[55] Sometimes, Lonesome made money at the games by "carrying that monkey box around, selling popcorn, peanuts, anything they told me to sell so long as it was legal." Lonesome also recalled people gambling at the games. "I'd see dollar bills and coins change hands. People were betting on what the batter would do, like get a hit or make an out."[56] Gambling was not limited to Elites games. Clinton "Butch" McCord remembered seeing black people with "buckets of money," during the games in Nashville, betting that the batter wouldn't "hit it out." "And they didn't mean 'hit it out of the park,'" McCord said. "They meant hit it out of the infield."[57]

Frank Lynch, a sports writer with the *Baltimore News American* and *Baltimore Sun* remembered blacks and whites sitting in different parts of the Bugle Field grandstand. "The blacks," Lynch said, "preferred the covered part of the seats behind home plate and the whites all sat in the bleachers along the baselines."[58] George Henderson, baseball coach for the Community College of Baltimore County, Essex, from 1984 through 2006, recalled seeing lots of whites at Bugle Field in the late 1940s. "Sometimes it was 50–50. They didn't have segregated seating but a lot of people sat with their own race." Henderson did not recall any incidents in the stands. "It wasn't an unruly crowd. It was a good time."[59] Charlotte Harvey, the wife of Elite pitcher Bill Harvey, agreed. "It was a nice crowd," she said. "There were very few arguments, among the fans that is. I'd get a ride there with someone or take the old 27 bus line. Vernon Green always had my ticket, which I think cost 25 cents, in an envelope for a box seat right behind home plate."[60]

For black and white patrons, the stands were none too comfortable. Lonesome remembered the stands as "rickety things like you'd see at the circus. If it rained, you just got wet, that's all."[61] Irving Morris, a Baltimore native who worked for Bethlehem Steel for thirty-three years and went mostly to weekend games, because he worked the night shift, concurred. "The place," said Morris, "had wooden fences and bleachers which were a rough place to sit. It wasn't comfortable at all."[62] Thomas Cripps[63] and several of his teammates on a team of seventeen-year-olds played a seven-inning game in 1948 before an Elites–New York Cubans contest. Cripps recounts that they decided not to shower after their game. The shower floor was earthen or covered with sawdust and he remembered it "as having a primitive look to it."[64] "The lights were so bad," Frank Lynch said, that during night games, "if a ball got up the alley between the outfielders, you'd lose sight of both the ball and the outfielder."

The edge of the outfield sloped up to meet a wooden fence that stood "ten to fifteen feet high."[65] Gaps in the clapboard outfield fence were plentiful. Ads pasted or tacked onto the fence touted the products of companies like Arrow Beer, Esskay Franks, Pepsi Cola, and American Beer.[66]

Other players did not always find Bugle Field to their liking either. The Elites' all-star shortstop Tommy "Pee Wee" Butts had problems with the playing surface. "They only had two groundskeepers," Butts said, "so it was hard to keep the grounds up. I'd go out myself and look around for bad spots . . . The ground was pretty bad, just a little too sandy, but there wasn't anybody who got his eyes put out . . . I guess we were pretty lucky."[67] McCord remembered Bugle Field as having a distant right field fence but a shorter left field fence, "where a guy like me could hit one over once in awhile."[68]

From 1938 to 1949 Richard Powell leased Bugle Field for the Elites from Matt Reinhold, by now an employee of the Gallagher Realty Company, which had bought the field from Cambria in 1938. Gallagher Realty was owned by Edward J. Gallagher, who, with fellow developers Ephraim Macht, Frank Novak, and James Keelty, built brick row houses in Baltimore's northern and western suburbs. The houses beckoned to people wanting to escape congestion, industrialization, and the presence of minority and ethnic groups thought to be inferior or threatening. Many of the row houses were built along the Route 40 corridor running westward from Howard Street, downtown.[69]

Having found a home field, albeit uncomfortable to both spectator and player, Wilson turned his attention to the team.

The Roster

In 1938, the year they came to Baltimore, the Elite Giants consisted of a group of young, for the most part southern-born, players. Player-manager and future Hall of Famer Raleigh "Biz" Mackey, a catcher, at 41 years of age and third baseman Felton Snow at 33 were the seniors. Philadelphia-born rookie catcher and future Hall of Famer Roy Cam-

Bugle Field as it appeared in 1942

panella, a mere 16, was the youngest and the only one born north of the Mason-Dixon Line.

Mackey, a native of Eagle Pass, Texas, had a first-rate baseball mind and the baseball tools to match. He thwarted steal attempts without rising from his squat. He hit well over .300. He played and managed for thirty years and was the best receiver in the Negro leagues during his prime. Mackey developed Campanella into a Hall of Fame catcher.[70] Mackey enjoyed his work. Buck Leonard, future Hall of Fame first baseman for the Homestead Grays, remembered Mackey as "a jovial fellow and full of fun, who always had something funny to say. When you went up to bat he'd try to distract you by saying things like, 'Hey, what kind of bat are you using. Ump, look at his bat. I don't think it's legal.' Or, 'I hear you're hitting over .400. Let's see how much you can hit today.'"[71] Mackey likely got his nickname by always giving batters "the biz."

Campanella met Mackey in the spring of 1938. Tom Dixon, a catcher for the Atlantic City Bacharachs, for whom Campanella was playing on weekends, introduced the two outside the Woodside Hotel at 141st Street and Broadway in Harlem. The Woodside, Dixon told the teenager, was "*the* place in Harlem for Negroes." Mackey asked Campanella if he wanted to join the Elites. Campanella said he did, and the two met the following week at the Attucks Hotel in Philadelphia. There Mackey gave the kid an Elites uniform and a contract for $60 a month.[72]

The older man took the teenager in tow. "He just asked me to sit beside him," Campanella said. "He helped me to learn everything. I tried to be the image of Biz Mackey. He was the master." On how to handle pitchers, Mackey told Campanella, "You got to scold some. You got to flatter some. You got to bribe some. You've got to think for some, and you got to mother them all. If you can do all those things, son, you'll be the biggest man in the league."[73]

Campanella learned to do all those things but the learning did not come easily. "Biz wasn't satisfied for me to do just one or two things good," Campanella said. "He wanted me to do everything good. And the onliest way I was going to improve myself was by working at the game, working, working, working. There were times when Biz made me cry with his constant dogging. But nobody ever had a better teacher."[74]

One needed a good teacher to develop into a star catcher in the Negro leagues, for as Campanella described the challenge behind the plate, "Anything went . . . Spit balls, shine balls, emery balls; pitchers used any and all of them. They nicked and moistened and treated the ball to make it flutter, and spin, dip, and break. Not only were there no rules against it, there weren't enough spare baseballs around to substitute clean, unmarked ones for the damaged ones, like they did in the big leagues. I was never sure what a ball would do once it left the pitcher's hand, even when he threw what I had called for. A man could get hurt catching in the colored league."[75]

While crediting Mackey with teaching him to catch, Campanella gave Tom Dixon credit for inspiring him, at age 15, by saying, "Let this stick in the bones of your head if nothing else I tell you does. Don't see yourself small. If you start off aiming small, you'll always be small . . . Remember, success ain't gonna chase you. You got to go after it."[76]

First baseman James "Red" Moore roomed with Campanella in 1939 and 1940. "In Baltimore, we stayed at the York Hotel—two to a room, Campy and me. I was a little older than Camp, but we got along really good." Moore remembered that Campanella's father took an active interest in his son's career. "His daddy would come to Baltimore and Philly and ride in the bus with us when we had games nearby."[77] Campanella's father also sat behind home plate during games at Bugle Field to yell encouragement to his son.[78]

Veterans manned the infield. In addition to Moore, James "Shifty" West was at first, Sammy T. Hughes at second, Felton Snow at third, and Jesse "Hoss" Walker at short. West, an eighteen-year veteran of the Negro leagues and native of Mobile, Alabama, played for Wilson in Nashville, Columbus, and Washington, as well as Baltimore. He was a hard-hitting, smooth-fielding first baseman who was elected twice to play in the East-West All-Star Classic, an annual game designed to showcase the talents of the best players from the Negro National League (NNL) and the Negro American League (NAL).[79] (By 1937, the NNL was composed of eastern teams and the NAL of midwestern and southern teams.) Calling him one of the best "grandstanders in the business," *Afro-American* sportswriter Art Carter said of West, "His antics around first base are a treat, and fans go just to watch him cavort around the initial bag."[80]

Sammy T. Hughes, a five-time all-star second baseman from Louisville, Kentucky, where he made his debut with the Louisville White Sox in 1929, played for Wilson's Elites in Nashville, Detroit, Columbus, Washington, and Baltimore. Tall and graceful, he was considered the best second baseman of his day.[81] Carter said of Hughes's play, "When one sees Hughes in action, they're looking upon a major leaguer. Sammy has all the grace of a [Charles] Gehringer [Detroit Tigers Hall of Fame second baseman] and the arm of a [Joe] Gordon [New York Yankee second baseman]. He is a daring base runner and will get more than his share of base hits. If it's number 5 then you're gazing at the best keystone sacker in Negro ball."[82] Fellow second baseman Dick Seay remembered Hughes as "a nice fellow. He wasn't one of those guys that was drinking and all. He'd stay in the hotel and go get his girl and visit with her."[83]

Snow, from Oxford, Alabama, first played with several teams in Louisville, Kentucky. He joined the Elites in 1933. Carter described Snow as "a consistent hitter and . . . the most dangerous batter on the team in the clutch. Though not flashy, he is a sure fielder and a great thrower."[84]

Snow also showed talent behind the wheel of the team bus when, somewhere in Pennsylvania's Allegheny Mountains in 1938, the brakes failed. Peering into the postmidnight darkness, Snow avoided a crash by steering the bus, then doing about 70 miles per hour, up a rutted side road into a farmer's field. The players breathed a sigh of relief only to be greeted by a red-faced farmer with shotgun in hand. On learning what happened, the farmer said he was thankful no one was hurt and lowered his gun.[85]

Hoss Walker, a native of Austin, Texas, made the most of his modest abilities to forge a twenty-two-year career as a shortstop and manager for seven teams. For ten of those years he was with the Elites in Nashville, Detroit, Columbus, Washington, then Baltimore. His steady fielding and baseball knowledge made up for weak hitting.[86]

Henry Kimbro, Burnis "Wild Bill" Wright, and Bill Hoskins patrolled the outfield.[87] Kimbro hailed from Nashville. "Kimmie," as he was known, was the best centerfielder of his day.[88] Noted for letting his bat, arm, and glove do the talking for him, Kimbro said little. When asked years later why he was so quiet, he replied, "I couldn't always find the right words for what I wanted to say."[89] Buck Leonard, not knowing Kimbro's struggle with words, found Kimbro hard to get along with, saying, "It seemed he was moody all the time."[90]

Wild Bill Wright, so nicknamed for his control problems as a teenage pitcher for his hometown Milan (Tennessee) Buffaloes, consistently hit over .300 in his ten years with the Elites and led them to a championship in 1939 with a league-leading .488 average. He had a powerful, if not always accurate, arm.[91] And he was fast. He was once clocked at 13.2 seconds in a race around the bases. "You'd get a single," teammate Lonnie Summers said, "and you knew Bill would get from first to third in a flash."[92] In 1943 he edged out future Hall of Famer Ray Dandridge to win the "Triple Crown" in Mexico where he played for more than ten years before being inducted into the Mexican Baseball Hall of Fame.

Considered by some a dirty ballplayer, Wright could be mean and temperamental. His temper probably saved the life of his Mexican League teammate, pitcher Rufus Lewis. Lewis was knocked unconscious after Lorenzo Cabrera, who took exception to being hit by a Lewis pitch, hit Lewis in the head with a bat. Before Cabrera could strike Lewis a second time, Wright was out of the dugout, bat in hand, and knocked Cabrera unconscious.[93] Buck Leonard remembered Wright as a mean ballplayer "who didn't carry on with a lot of fun and jokes like some of the rest of the ballplayers did." Wright showed his mean side by striking an umpire during a 1939 Elites–Grays game and insisting on playing the next day even though he had been fined 25 dollars and suspended for three games. Wright's stubbornness caused the game to be forfeited to the Grays.[94] Wright appeared as a surprise guest on television's *This Is Your Life* when the show featured Campanella in 1958; he was Campanella's first roommate with the Elites.[95]

Bill Hoskins, born in Charleston, Mississippi, and known as an average fielder, added his .300-plus batting average and speed on the bases to the Elites' attack from 1938 to 1946. He played briefly with several other teams both before and after his time with the Elites.[96]

The core of the Elites' pitching staff in 1938 consisted of the "big three," Andy "Pullman" Porter, Jonas Gaines, and Bill Byrd. Porter, from Little Rock, Arkansas, pitched for the Elites from 1932 to 1946 with five of those years spent on the mound in Mexico. He made his debut with the Louisville Black Caps in 1932 and joined Wilson's Nashville Elites later that year. His best season for the Elites was 1942, when he went 7 and 0 with two shutouts. He was a sharp dresser with a weakness for tailor-made suits.[97]

Byrd, from Canton, Georgia, led the staff in wins from 1938 until his release in 1950. He appeared in five East-West All-Star Games; the only pitchers to appear in more were future Hall of Famers Leon Day and Hilton Smith with six appearances apiece. The last Negro league pitcher to legally throw the spitball, Byrd also had command of a knuckler, slider, roundhouse curve, and a sinker. He retired from baseball with a 114–72 record in league games.[98] Byrd chewed slippery elm; a soft,

Three Elites stars: (left to right) *Burnis "Wild Bill" Wright, Andy "Pullman" Porter, Sammy T. Hughes*

greenish-colored bark, to help his ball do tricks. Campanella called him "Daddy," because he took an interest in young players, advising them on a number of matters.[99]

Jonas Gaines, born in New Roads, Louisiana, rounded out the "Big Three." A graduate of Southern University, he made his debut with the Newark Eagles in 1937. He pitched for the Elites from 1938 to 1948, taking three years out for military service and one for a year in Mexico. Selected for three East-West All-Star squads, he chose from a fastball, curveball, slider, change, and screwball. He played in Japan for the 1953 season, one of the first Americans to play for a Japanese team.[100]

Wilson now had a team of veteran players and a receptive city.

Hard Landing

The Elites opened spring training in Wilson Park on April 2, 1938, in Nashville. Infielder George Scales arrived a few days later from the New York Black Yankees in exchange for infielder Leroy Morney. Scales took over the skipper's duties from Mackey, who had managed the team the year before in Washington, allowing Mackey to catch full time.

Spring training lasted only a week. Limited funds meant little time for getting in shape before playing before paying customers. As Campanella put it, "Play yourself into shape! That was the only way the Negro leagues got on the ball. Man, we didn't just sop up sun and orange juice and run laps and play 'pepper' and listen to theory on the 'pick-off' play [as he would do during spring training with the Brooklyn Dodgers]. No sir—regular exhibition games with the hat being passed."[101]

With twenty players on board, the Elites started the exhibition season by playing the Memphis Red Sox of the Negro American League in Memphis on Palm Sunday. The Elites lost the game 6–5, their first in Baltimore Elite Giants uniforms.[102] The blue-gray flannels sported red piping and the name "Elite Giants" in red letters across the front. A player's number was on the back of his uniform in red.[103] A large red letter "B" would be added to the left sleeve in later years.

The team's four errors during the Memphis game attested to the Elites' not being fully rounded into shape. The Red Sox scored three runs on just one hit in the first inning, but the Elites rallied in later frames to make the game interesting.[104] However, the Elites did well enough that spring for one observer to call them "on paper, the team to beat for the pennant. It is the best balanced team in the loop. Every man is experienced and seasoned."[105]

The prophecy went unfulfilled. By June 11, the Elites were at 5–6 in league play, good for fourth place in the NNL standings behind the Homestead Grays, the Philadelphia Stars, and the Pittsburgh Crawfords.[106] The Elites then lost six more games in league play. One of the losses came before 15,000 fans in Yankee Stadium on Sunday, June 26. Team owners Wilson, Greenlee (Crawfords), and James Semler (New York Black Yankees) had arranged for a four-team doubleheader that

Elites pitcher Jonas Gaines

day involving their teams and the Philadelphia Stars. Four-team double-headers on Sundays in large stadiums guaranteed a large turnout. The date for this contest was no doubt selected with the knowledge that many attending the Joe Louis–Max Schmeling heavyweight bout on June 22 in Yankee Stadium, where Louis knocked Schmeling out in round one, would stay over for the games. In their game, the Elites took a 7–5 lead into the bottom half of the ninth only to see the Craws score three runs to win the game 8–7.

The first half of the season ended on July 4th. Independence Day and Labor Day usually marked the end of the halves of the season. The Elites finished the first half in fifth place, out of seven teams, with a 12–14 record. The Grays finished in first place, at 26–6.[107]

The Elites stumbled through the second half of the season. An indication of their struggles is that they dropped a game 5–1 to the lowly Washington Black Senators a week later at home.[108] The Senators were in last place and folded before the season was over. The Elites ended their first season on a positive note, however, by taking an end-of-the-season Labor Day doubleheader from the Philadelphia Stars 4–3 and 12–9.[109]

In the tradition of inconsistent recordkeeping that characterized the Negro leagues, records for the second-half standings are nonexistent. Full-time scorekeepers were another staple of the major leagues that the Negro leagues could not afford. Gus Greenlee, owner of the Crawfords and president of the NNL, and Cum Posey, owner of the Grays, filed a report giving the second-half order of finish as Grays in first place followed by the Stars, Crawfords, Elites, Eagles, and Yankees. How they arrived at the standings is not known. They did not provide a won-lost record for any of the teams in their report. In their words, "Sportswriters didn't receive league news because the various club secretaries did not send in the scores to the secretary of the league."[110] Their ruling pleased

Three Elite Giants on the 1938 All-Star East squad. Sammy T. Hughes is fourth from the left, back row; "Wild Bill" Wright is to Hughes's left; and "Biz" Mackey is to Wright's left.

the Grays. They won the 1938 Negro National League crown by finishing first in both halves of the season.

After that first year, Tom Wilson decided to keep the Elites in Baltimore. The box office had been good to him even if the team's won-loss record had disappointed. Three of the Elites—Hughes, Wright, and Mackey—won election to the East squad for the East-West All-Star Game.

CHAPTER 2

Pennants and Jumpers

Elites Take It All

Resolved to improve on the results of their maiden season in Baltimore, the Elites opened spring training on April 2, 1939, once again in Nashville. Tom Wilson appointed Felton Snow to manage the team while retaining his duties at third base,[1] and George Scales returned to the New York Black Yankees as their manager for 1939.[2] Three pitchers from the Elites' squad, Andy Porter, Robert "Schoolboy" Griffith, and Jimmy Direaux, found more promising opportunities in the Mexican leagues and "jumped" their Elite contracts. Booking agents Gottlieb and Smith had better luck getting Oriole Park in 1939. The field's owners permitted the team to play occasional doubleheaders there when the O's were on the road.

The major leagues' exclusion of blacks had the effect of capping Negro leaguers' salaries far below those paid to white players of the same and even less talent. While the discrepancy between major league and Negro league salaries was substantial, players for the Elites fared better economically than did much of Baltimore's black workforce, most of whom held low-paying jobs. Rookies took home at least $60 a month while the stars could command $300 and more a month. Many of the players used their earnings to dress well in custom-made suits, fedoras, and spit-polished shoes.[3] Even so, many a star Negro leaguer "jumped" his contract in the States for one in Mexico, Puerto Rico, Venezuela, the

Dominican Republic, or Cuba. Players could not ignore the chance to double or triple their salary in a country whose populace adored baseball players of any pigmentation.

Owners were powerless to stop the contract violations, even though they voted often to ban the offending players for periods of time ranging from three to five years. But when a Campanella, a Byrd, or a Wright, who filled many a seat at Bugle Field and elsewhere, wanted to return to the States, the owners could not afford to abide by their bans. A player might have to pay a $100 fine or sit out a week or two to suit up, thereby allowing owners to save some face.

To generate the needed revenue, Wilson scheduled as many games, league and non-league or barnstorming, as possible. By contrast, major league clubs played a fixed schedule in which each team faced every other team in their league twenty-two times a year. Negro league owners drew up a schedule of games for the season at their winter meetings, but the schedule was not set in concrete, as is shown by a letter Effa Manley wrote to Vernon Green on July 17, 1939:

> We have completed arrangements for the Eagles-Elites in Federal Park, Easton, Md. Tuesday, July 25th and Gordy Park, Salisbury, Md. Wednesday, July 26th.
>
> I am writing Gottlieb now to tell him the 27th and 29th are still open; he may probably be able to put us in Wilmington or some other place . . . In the meantime I will see you in Richmond Friday night the 21st.
>
> We have also been unable to get anything for Saturday, the 22nd, so I guess we will be open that day.

The impromptu scheduling made for long and frequent bus rides, the Negro leagues' primary mode of transportation. Major leaguers traveled in comfy Pullman train cars and later by air. Campanella said of life on the Elites' bus, "We traveled in a big bus and many's the time we never bothered to take off our uniforms going from one place to another . . . The bus was our home, dressing room, dining room, and hotel."[4]

The ongoing scheduling of games demanded endurance from the players. Campanella, for instance, once caught four games in a single day.

Elites pitcher Robert "Schoolboy" Griffith

The first two were a midday doubleheader in Cincinnati, Ohio, and the last two, also a doubleheader, were played that evening 275 miles away in Youngstown, Ohio. Players rested up the best they could between games. They took care not to get hurt during games because, as Campanella declared, "if you did, you didn't get paid."[5]

With three of their star pitchers gone to Mexico, Wilson's men started the 1939 season poorly. Two weeks into the season the team had lost its first four games, while the Grays had won three of their first four.[6] Two of those wins for the Grays were, by one account, "ignominious losses"

Elites bus driver, Wilson Campbell, standing next to the team's bus, 1945

for the Elites. Before the opening day home crowd at Oriole Park on Sunday, May 19, in a doubleheader, the Grays trounced the Elites 7–1 in the opener and routed them 11–0 in the second game, which the umpires mercifully called after six innings to comply with the 6:00 p.m. Sunday curfew.[7]

One of the Elites' few wins in the first half of the 1939 season came on June 4th against the Cuban Stars before 12,000 fans at Yankee Stadium.[8] The win was the Elites' first in the newly created Jacob Ruppert Memorial Cup Tournament. New York Yankees president Edward Barrow began the tournament in 1939 to honor Yankees owner Jake Ruppert, who had died the previous year. Ruppert had opened Yankee Stadium to Negro league teams for the first time on July 5, 1930, when the New York Lincoln Elites squared off against the Baltimore Black Sox for a doubleheader. The games were played for the benefit of the Brotherhood of Sleeping Car Porters, led by A. Philip Randolph, later a prominent civil rights leader.[9]

The tournament consisted of five, four-team doubleheaders to be played on Sundays in the "House That Ruth Built." The team with the best record would receive a trophy and $500.[10] On July 2, the Elites were back in Yankee Stadium for round two of the Ruppert Cup tournament. They shut out the New York Black Yankees in the feature game of the doubleheader 4–0.[11] While faring well in Ruppert Cup competition, the Elites finished third for the first half of the season. The Grays again won the flag.

The Elites found new life as the second half got under way. They took four straight games from the Philadelphia Stars during the weekend of July 8–9. To help sustain their winning ways, the Elites picked up five players from the Atlanta Black Crackers in what was described by the press as "the biggest switch in players to be heralded in many seasons." Baltimore got James "Red" Moore, a fancy-fielding good-hitting first baseman; Tommy "Pee Wee" Butts; two pitchers, Ed Dixon and Felix Evans; and catcher Oscar Brown. To make room for the new players, the Elites sold first baseman Jim West to the Stars and Biz Mackey to the Eagles. Campanella had graduated from high school, and his play had improved to starting status. Brown was now available to back him up.[12]

Butts was the prize acquisition. He owned the shortstop position until 1951. Born in Sparta, Georgia, he made six appearances in the All-Star classic.[13] Lennie Pearson, long-time first baseman with the Newark Eagles and the Elites' player-manager for part of the 1950 season, said, "Butts was a tremendous shortstop and a pesky hitter. He could go behind second better than any man I ever saw in my life . . . He wasn't too old for the majors," Pearson added, "but he loved life, and when I say he loved life, I mean he loved life, especially the women. That may have hurt his chances [to make the majors]."[14] Good as he was, Pee Wee suffered from a case of rookie jitters in his first game for the Elites. "The first game I played," Butts recounted, "you know what happened? Well, you know how it is when you first start, you get shaky. Three balls in the grandstand. I mean I threw them in. I didn't hit them in."[15] Butts's jitters made him throw three balls over the first baseman's head and into the seats behind first base.

Although referred to as a "switch" in the papers, players were not exchanged for other players. The Atlanta Black Crackers started the 1939

Elites shortstop Thomas "Pee Wee" Butts ready for the ball

season playing in Indianapolis as the Indianapolis A.B.C.'s, but the team could not find a ballpark; so, Moore said, "the Black Crackers broke up and the five of us went to Baltimore after Baltimore contacted us."[16]

With their beefed-up infield and pitching staff, the Elites were in first place by early August with a 12–5 record. The Grays followed at 6–6.[17] The Elites kept the heat on the Grays and won the second half championship easily. Ordinarily, the winner of the first and second halves of the season, in this case the Grays and Elites, met in a playoff series to determine the season's pennant winner. But not in 1939. The four teams (out of six) that had won the most games throughout the season competed in a playoff series. More games meant more gate receipts, which may be what caused the owners to choose a four-team playoff. In any event, the Grays (33–14) were considered the league leaders and faced the fourth-place Philadelphia Stars (31–32). The second-place Eagles (29–20) met the third-place Elites (25–21).[18] The Elites survived the first round of the playoffs by beating the Eagles three games to one in the best-of-five series. The Elites' last two wins came before 5,000 fans at Oriole Park on September 10 in a Sunday doubleheader. They pounded out twenty-one hits, including one homer (Byrd's).[19] The Grays prevailed over the Stars, three games to two.

The finals opened in Philadelphia on Saturday, September 16, with the Grays winning a squeaker 2–1. The Elites retaliated with a 7–5 victory in the first game of a doubleheader the next day at Oriole Park. The win was attributed to "airtight support by both . . . infield and outfield, with Bill Wright and Henry Kimbro making sensational catches combined with timely clouting by Wright and Felton Snow." Jonas Gaines went the distance for the Elites, surviving a Josh Gibson home run over the left field fence. The second game ended in a 1–1 tie when the umpire's watch read 6:00 and the Sunday curfew went into effect. The series was tied 1–1.[20]

The teams traveled to Philadelphia for two games, one on Friday and one on Saturday, both at Parkside Field. The Grays took Friday's game by the narrow margin of 2–1. The Elites fared better on Saturday, beating the Grays 10–5. Campanella put on a show for his hometown fans with a homer, a double, and two singles while driving in five of the Elites' runs.

Byrd survived, giving up fifteen hits to the Grays, including three singles and a home run to Gibson. Luckily for the Elites, the bases were empty each time Gibson appeared at the plate.[21] The Elites' win tied the series at 2–2.

The teams went to Yankee Stadium the next day for the final game, before 10,000 fans. A stomach ailment sidelined Hughes just before game time. He was taken to Harlem Hospital for an examination but recovered in time to see the end of the game. Snow took Hughes's place at second while Hoss Walker filled in for Snow at third.

The game was scoreless through six innings. In the seventh, Wright doubled off Roy Partlow. Hoskins singled Wright home. Campanella sent Hoskins home with a single after Hoskins had advanced to second on an error.[22] Then Gaines loaded the bases with Grays by walking Harris, Gibson, and Leonard in the eighth. Player-manager Snow brought Willie "Bubber" Hubert out of the bullpen to pitch to Henry Spearman, who hit a weak pop-up. Hubert proceeded to set the Grays down in order in the ninth.[23] (Hubert's performance was the highlight of his brief career with the Elites [1939–1940]. An accomplished pitcher who was known for "cutting the ball to compensate for his lack of other legitimate pitches," he was difficult to handle both on and off the field.[24]) Jonas Gaines, in his best game of the year, had thrown a three-hit shutout until the eighth inning and got the 2–0 win. The Elites had won the Negro National League championship and the Jacob Ruppert Memorial Cup. Bill "Bojangles" Robinson, noted tap dancer and part owner of the New York Black Yankees, had thrown out the first ball, and afterward he presented the gold-plated Ruppert Memorial Trophy to a broadly smiling Tom Wilson surrounded by Elite players and officials.[25]

Controversy surrounded the championship long after the final out. Although the Grays' stationery for 1947 does not list 1939 as one of the team's pennant-winning years,[26] a Grays envelope postmarked January 19, 1949, and addressed to sportswriter Art Carter reads "1937–38–39–40–41–42–43–44–45" under the heading "Negro National League Champions."[27] Grays first baseman Buck Leonard took issue with the Elites' championship claim, saying, "We won the regular season pennant. We didn't have a split season like we did in previous years . . . so we decided

"Smiling Tom" Wilson, Elites players, and NNL officials pose with the Ruppert Cup trophy, Yankee Stadium, September 1939. Standing, left to right: *Bill Hoskins, Sammy T. Hughes, Vernon Green, Felton Snow, Doug Smith, Tom Wilson, James Semler (New York Black Yankees owner), Alex Pompez (New York Cubans owner), Frank Forbes (umpire)*. Kneeling, left to right: *Jonas Gaines, Henry Kimbro, Tom Glover, James Moore, Jesse Walker, Roy Campanella, Bill Bojangles Robinson, Chester Washington (*Pittsburgh Courier*), Willie Hubert, Bill Byrd, Ace Adams, Boogie Wolf, Wild Bill Wright, Pee Wee Butts.*

to have a four-team tourney in our league." He did not say to whom "we" referred, but as he recalled it, the tourney had nothing to do with determining the league championship. Leonard acknowledged that Baltimore won the tourney and the Ruppert Cup but objected to the Elites' basing their claim to being league champions on the fact that they won the Ruppert Cup. Leonard claimed that the Grays won the championship because they won the most games during the year.[28] Press accounts gave the championship to the Elites. The *Baltimore Afro-American* on September 30, 1939, stated, "Climaxing an uphill campaign in a blaze of glory, the Baltimore Elite Giants won the Negro National League baseball championship and the Jacob Ruppert Trophy by turning back the Homestead Grays . . . in the final game of the titular series at Yankee Stadium, Sunday." The *Chicago Defender* on July 6, 1940, in announcing an upcoming game between the Eagles and the Elites, said the Eagles would "clash with the league-leading Baltimore Elite Giants, champions of 1939."

The Elites had made good on their resolve to improve on the lackluster results of their first year in Baltimore, bringing home a Negro National League pennant, the city's first since that won by the Black Sox in 1929.

The controversy surrounding the Elites' 1939 pennant was but one of many controversies that beset the Negro National League during the Elites' stay in Baltimore. Wilson had a hand in many of them.

Owners Vie for Leadership

The owners' decision to substitute a playoff series for the traditional practice of the first- and second-half winners meeting to award the pennant was but one instance of the Negro league's flexible—some would say loose—structure. Such decisions were frequent. They stimulated hard feelings and criticism and were enabled, at times, by Wilson when he was NLL president.

NNL owners had elected Wilson to succeed Gus Greenlee as president at their winter meetings in Philadelphia in late February 1939.[29] Greenlee's financial problems forced him to take his Pittsburgh Crawfords out of the league and leave Pittsburgh in 1939; after several years of play in Toledo and Indianapolis he had to disband the team.[30] Grays owner Posey lauded Wilson's first-year performance saying, "Wilson has been a success as president of the Negro National League during his first year and should be re-elected. He has brought order out of chaos."[31]

Effa Manley, business manager of the Newark Eagles, disagreed. She saw Wilson as a playboy who put "having a little drink and a little fun" ahead of his baseball responsibilities.[32] Given their contrasting styles, Manley and Wilson could not help but clash. In a May 16, 1939, letter to Wilson, who was in Nashville tending to his ventures there, Effa wrote,

1939 Elite Giants, National Negro League champions

"This is the fourth letter I have written to you and received no answer to. I certainly hope you get this one and answer it right away." She laid out her concerns and suggestions about scheduling, publicity, and players jumping contracts. Two weeks later she received a telegram from Wilson that read, "Meet me in Gottlieb's office tonight to get things straightened out."[33] Effa declined. Gottlieb's office was in Philadelphia; Manley's was in Newark, New Jersey, 86 miles away.

Determined to remove Wilson from office, at the owners' 1940 winter meeting, Effa Manley had her husband, Abe, nominate C. B. Powell, a New York City physician and owner of the *New York Amsterdam News*, to be the NNL's commissioner. She made a similar proposal to Negro American League owners, suggesting they elect Judge William H. Hastie, dean of Howard University's law school in Washington, D.C., as the league's commissioner to replace J. B. Martin. In support of Powell she said, "The Negro National League needs a business man . . . who can step in and organize, direct, and make decisions when they should be made. Such a man is Dr. C. B. Powell who has no axe to grind for himself or for any individual club or owner."[34]

Both Wilson and Martin informed the Manleys that neither league was ready for a change in leadership, and both men said they would not vote for Effa's candidates. Effa got the same response to her proposal that the NNL owners elect the *Chicago Defender*'s New York editor, Al Monroe, as secretary in place of Posey.[35] During one of the most tumultuous league meetings, Effa's proposals prompted the normally laid-back Wilson to fume that he was "infuriated by the secretive manner in which a few of the members attempted to oust me." Wilson came close to tears when the Black Yankees' James Semler cast a vote against him.[36] Alex Pompez, owner of the New York Cubans, joined with Effa and Semler and voted for Powell. That meant three votes for the Powell-Monroe ticket. Posey of the Grays and Ed Gottlieb of the Stars voted for Wilson, who voted for himself. The owners resolved the impasse by agreeing that the 1939 officers would stay put for the 1940 season.[37]

Effa Manley was not the only one who wanted Wilson out of office. Sportswriter Randy Dixon took Wilson to task for "never giving your umpires a single instruction, for pocketing so much money from the East-West Game [in which Wilson had a financial interest] the year before thereby confusing folks with logical minds and making them think a racket is brewing beneath their noses." Dixon suggested that Wilson "invoke at least one league rule to justify your existence and ordain that overalls and gas masks be distributed along with each ticket at the league's park in Philly where nostalgic kayos emanate from the neighboring railroad yards."[38] *Pittsburgh Courier* sports editor Wendell Smith said of Wilson, "If he had any great fault it was his habit of literally disappearing at times when his presence was necessary. At times, he was harder to find than a snowball in the tropics."[39]

Manley did not give up. Prior to the 1942 NNL league meetings, she wrote to Cum Posey asking him to "*please* get Tom out of there this year. It is really tragic to have a business as big as this run by someone like Tom . . . I really wish Abe [her husband and Eagles' co-owner] were the chairman. One thing sure. We couldn't be any worse."[40] Effa's request went unanswered.

She continued, nevertheless, to keep the heat on Wilson. She wrote

Wilson on August 23, 1943, the day after Posey and Semler on their own authority changed a game from an exhibition game, which did not count in the standings, to a league game, which did count. "If this can be allowed," Manley wrote, "there is nothing to prevent two teams from getting together and doing anything. Especially a weak one and a strong one. I would appreciate an answer from you as to what you think is right."[41] Wilson's response could not be found.

The dispute over which team won the 1944 second-half NNL flag was another example of how Wilson sanctioned owners' arbitrary decisions by his inaction. This time, Posey claimed that the second game of a Labor Day doubleheader in Detroit, which the Grays lost to the New York Cubans, was an exhibition game, not a league game. Had the second game counted as a league game, the Philadelphia Stars, and not the Grays, would have won the flag. Both games were scheduled league games and should have counted as such. Oliver "Butts" Brown, writing in the *Newark Herald* about Posey and Semler's side deal, said, "It is time for Tom Wilson to be the President of the league or step down and let someone else function."[42] Sportswriter Rollo Wilson, who served as NNL commissioner in 1934, weighed in with the observation that Wilson had "outlived his usefulness as president . . . if indeed he was ever of real service to any save himself and a favored few."[43] An article in the *Amsterdam News* called Posey's act "one of the most high-handed procedures in the history of the sport." The same article reprinted a letter from Philadelphia Stars co-owner Ed Bolden to Wilson imploring Wilson to take action.[44] Wilson took no action.

Wilson's unwillingness to answer letters unless they were related to the East-West All-Star Game was well known.[45] He had a financial stake in the game, which may explain his attentiveness to correspondence about it. Wilson may have helped initiate the game. Lucius Harper, writing in 1939 for the *Chicago Defender*, credited Greenlee, Wilson, and Chicago American Giants' owner R. A. Cole with initiating the game.[46] Negro league historian Larry Lester, citing a 1942 article in the *Pittsburgh Courier*, reported that two sportswriters, Roy Sparrows of the *Pittsburgh Sun-Telegraph* and Bill Nunn of the *Pittsburgh Courier* had approached

Greenlee with the idea for the game. Greenlee had suggested they contact Cole about using Comiskey Park, which they did. The article did not mention Wilson.

Wilson's financial interest in the game changed over time. In 1933, '34, and '35, he was one of three "benefactors" (Greenlee and Cole being the other two) who divided the proceeds of the game equally among themselves. Starting in 1936, all teams in both leagues shared equally in the receipts.[47] Later, Martin and Wilson each took 10 percent of the gate in lieu of salary for their league president duties.[48]

Wilson, though ineffectual in the eyes of some and a partner in flexibility in the eyes of others, laid down the law when he saw fit to do so. In May of 1941, Semler plucked Satchel Paige away from the Negro American League's Kansas City Monarchs to pitch for his Negro National League New York Black Yankees in their May 11 opener against the Philadelphia Stars. Perhaps remembering Semler's vote against him a year earlier, Wilson said he was incensed by Semler's action and fined him an undisclosed amount. Wilson proposed to NAL president Martin that such actions in the future be grounds for suspending the offending player as well as fining the owner. Martin agreed.[49]

Wilson faced a similar situation in 1942 when the Cleveland Buckeyes, also of the Negro American League, offered two of his own Elites, Roy Campanella and Sammy Hughes, $250 to "jump" the Elites for a couple of days to play in one game for the Buckeyes. Both men played in the game, against Wilson's orders not to. He suspended them for thirty days, leveled a fine of $250 against each, and denied Campanella permission to play in the East-West All-Star Game, to which he had been elected.[50]

Campanella claims that he did play in the 1942 East-West game and that he only got in the game because the fans were yelling for him. Wilson, according to Campanella, "got in the last dig" by putting him at third. In fact, Campanella may have been in Chicago, where the game was happening, but he did not play.[51] Biographer Milton Shapiro adds to the myth with more detail: "As Roy trotted back to the bench, he nodded at the West's team shortstop, who was taking the field. It was the first time Roy had seen the man, though he had heard about him.

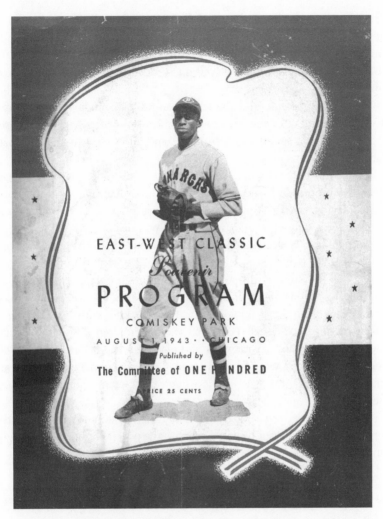

Leroy Robert "Satchel" Paige as a Kansas City Monarch on the cover of the 1943 East–West game program

The player was Jackie Robinson." Campanella could not have nodded at Robinson during that game, as neither man was in the line-up. Nods might have been exchanged during the *1945* game, when both were in the line-up. Robinson only played one year in the Negro leagues, 1945, for the Kansas City Monarchs.[52]

Miffed by the fine and the suspension, Campanella took up Jorge Pasquel, president of the Mexican League, on his offer to play in Mexico. Campanella spent the rest of 1942 and all of 1943 in the Mexican League.

Wilson also acted when he thought the Negro leagues' image had been compromised. In 1942 he penned an order banning all NNL clubs from playing the Ethiopian Clowns, whose practice of painting their faces and literally clowning on the field was deemed by Wilson to be "detrimental to Negro league baseball." All clubs in both leagues agreed to observe the ban.[53]

Wilson did step up his support for umpires. Grays player Jud Wilson felt Tom Wilson's ire in 1944 to the tune of a $25 fine and a three-game suspension for striking umpire Phil Cockrell with his bat after a disputed third strike call. (Cockrell was not injured.)[54] In 1945, when George Scales, a former manager and player for the Elites, twice pulled the Black Yankees, whom he was managing, off the field to dispute an umpire's call, Wilson levied a $500 fine on the team and a $50 fine on Scales.[55]

Though not decisive enough to satisfy Effa Manley and several sportswriters, Wilson showed he could exercise the powers of his office, if only on a selective basis.

Jumpers, Trades, and Close Finishes

As the 1940 season got under way, Hitler's war machine was in high gear, and the prospect of American men of baseball age being drafted became a possibility. War in Europe had begun as the 1939 season drew to a close. The United States, while supplying the Allied powers with materials through the Cash and Carry and the Lend-Lease Acts, stayed out of direct involvement in the war in Europe until December 11, 1941, when Hitler declared war on the United States. Four days earlier, the Japanese attack on Pearl Harbor had brought the country into the Pacific War. On the Elites baseball front in 1940 and 1941 there would also be close pennant races, several trades, and the loss of key players to the jingle of pesos.

One trade rumor had Elites fans on the edge of their preseason seats. Reports out of the same 1940 owners meeting that almost ousted Wilson as NNL president had Josh Gibson coming to Baltimore. In exchange, the Grays would receive Felton Snow and Sammy T. Hughes. Another rumor had former Elites manager George Scales returning to the Elites from the New York Black Yankees in exchange for shortstop Hoss Walker and pitcher Al Johnson.[56] The rumors were only partially true. Scales returned to the Elites in a trade for Walker and Johnson, but as a player only. Snow retained his manager's role. Hughes stayed in Baltimore. Gibson played in Venezuela.

Gibson was not the only player to head to Latin America. Three of the Elites' stalwarts, pitcher Bill Byrd, slugger "Wild Bill" Wright, and fastball pitcher Tom Glover, all headed south as well—Byrd to Venezuela and Wright and Glover to Mexico.[57] Responding to criticism for his decision to jump the team, Byrd said, "They treat you better down there. They pay your way down. Get you an apartment and pay you pretty well . . . They roll out the red carpet for you."[58]

The remaining Elites opened spring training on March 24 in New Orleans, where they took the luxury of two weeks to work out before hitting the road. Two new pitchers, "Ace" Adams and Clarence Williams, won jobs on the starting rotation.

In a ceremony before the opening day doubleheader with the Philadelphia Stars got under way, Wilson presented each member of the 1939 team with a watch for winning the 1939 NNL championship and put the Ruppert Cup Trophy on display at Oriole Park.[59] Marse S. Callaway, a prominent black real estate broker who was active in the Republican Party, threw out the first ball.[60] A combination of heavy hitting and good pitching by the Elites and sloppy fielding (twelve errors) by the Stars resulted in two wins for the Elites, 6–1 and 5–2.[61]

Three games between the Elites and the Grays at the end of May were harbingers of the close 1940 pennant race to come. The teams split a doubleheader at Griffith Stadium on Sunday, May 19. The Grays got off to a quick 3–0 lead in the first inning of game one, thanks to singles by Jerry Benjamin and Vic Harris and a towering Buck Leonard homer. Elite pitcher "Ace" Adams, dubbed in the press a "diminutive southpaw," then settled down, allowing only two hits until the eighth inning, when he gave up two more runs. The Elites managed only six hits and two runs, losing 7–2. The Elites bested the Grays 8–5 in the nightcap, though, thanks to a two-run triple by Campanella, a one-run double by Snow, and two singles by Scales. The Elites edged the Grays 9–8 the next day in Harrisburg, Pennsylvania. Campanella had two homers, Leonard hit another tape-measure job, but Scales put the game away for the Elites with a two-run pinch-hit homer in the eighth.[62]

The wins sent the Elites into June in first place, a position they clung to until the last week of June, when their fortunes headed south. An 8–6 loss to the New York Black Yankees in the first of two games at Oriole Park before 5,000 fans on Sunday, June 23, was the first of two critical losses. Even though the Elites bounced back to take game two 4–3, due largely to the wildness of Yankees pitchers John "Neck" Stanley and Robert Evans,[63] their loss to Newark a week later, also at Oriole Park, put the Elites a game behind the Homestead Grays. There the first half ended.[64]

The Elites jumped into the lead early in the second half with two wins over the Grays in a twin bill at Oriole Park before 4,000 fans on July 14. "Ace" Adams, now the ace of the staff in both name and performance, limited the Grays to three hits in game one, while his mates smashed fourteen hits for twelve runs, led by Campanella, Hoskins, and Hughes, who each homered. Game two was closer but not much of a contest as the Elites prevailed 9–3, managing to complete the game before the 6:00 p.m. curfew.[65]

The Elites and the Grays met again on Sunday, July 28, at Yankee Stadium, tied at 4–4 in head-to-head contests for the season. Each team won one game, allowing the Elites to keep a two-game lead over the Grays. Ray Brown kept the Elites to three hits in game one with his knuckleball and a change-up, bringing his record to 12 wins and no losses with a 5–0 win. With Brown off the mound in game two, the Elites did better, winning by the volleyball score of 15–6. They hammered the Grays' pitching staff for eleven extra-base hits on their way to an eighteen-hit total. Butts had a perfect four-for-four day. Scales punched out two doubles. Bud Barbee, Nate Moreland, and Bill Perkins each tripled, as did Snow. Adams went the distance.[66]

The Elites' undoing came at a doubleheader with the Grays on Sunday, September 1, at Griffith Stadium. The Grays played both games under protest. They thought Kimbro should have been suspended for a fight he started a week earlier. Wilson, as NNL president, ruled otherwise.

Ace Adams was in top form for most of the first game. Through seven innings, he allowed the Grays only three singles in a scoreless duel against Ray Brown. Adams gave himself a one-run cushion by scoring from third on a sacrifice fly by Kimbro. The Grays figured Adams out in the eighth inning, scoring six runs to win the game 6–1. The teams were now tied. In the second game, thanks to solid pitching by Bud Barbee and timely hitting by Perkins, Moore, and Hughes, the Elites took a 5–4 lead into the bottom of the seventh, with the 6:00 p.m. curfew approaching. As the eighth began, the Grays' Dave Whatley struck out, but Vic Harris and Howard Easterling tallied for the Grays, putting men on first and second. With Buck Leonard at the plate, Elites manager Snow relieved Barbee, bringing in southpaw James "Lefty" Reese, who forced Leonard to hit a slow roller to Hughes at second for the second out. Hometown Washingtonian Jud Wilson ended the suspense when, in the words of sportswriter Sam Lacy, he "poked a bewhiskered drive in the well-known Dick Merriwell fashion" into the deep corner in right field to score the winning run.[67] The Grays did not need their protest and now led the Elites by one game, a lead they never relinquished.

The Elites won their second Ruppert Cup by defeating the New York Cubans in the opening game of a non-league doubleheader a week later at Yankee Stadium.[68] While Monumental City fans were pleased that the Ruppert Cup stayed in Baltimore, they no doubt wondered what might have been had Wright, Glover, and Byrd stayed in Baltimore.

1940 Elites' infield: left to right, *George Scales, Pee Wee Butts, Felton Snow, Red Moore, and Sammy T. Hughes*

1940 Elites' outfield: left to right, *Bill Hoskins, Jimmie Armistead, Norman Robinson, and Henry Kimbro*

Surely their talents could have tipped the balance enough times for the Elites to have come out ahead in the tight race of 1940.

Anticipating that NNL owners would lift a three-year ban on players who had jumped their teams to play in Mexico, Wilson and Semler announced an eleven-player trade on January 2, 1941. Seven Elites— Kimbro, catcher Bill Perkins, and pitchers Bud Barbee, Charles "Spec" Roberts, Bob Griffith, Tom Parker, and Willie Hubert—would go to the Yankees. In return, the Elites would get catcher Robert Clarke, outfielder Charley Biot, third baseman Henry Spearman, and right-handed pitcher Jesse Brown. It was clear to all that the trade would improve a struggling Yankee team but the trade of five Elites pitchers, according to an *Afro-American* reporter "set tongues wagging about the owner's intentions."[69]

To the relief of Elite fans, the trade went through but not as reported. In an unusual move, the NNL owners declined to lift the ban at their January meeting, making Roberts, Griffith, Hubert, and Parker ineligible to play for any Negro league team in 1941. Wilson and Semler refashioned the deal so that Perkins, Kimbro, and Barbee went to the Yankees in exchange for Biot, Clarke, Roy Williams, and Spearman.[70]

NAL owners did not agree with the decision to keep the ban in place. Owners of both leagues took up the debate over the ban during their joint meeting in the last week of February in Chicago at the Grand Hotel. Following a 6–6 vote along league lines, they compromised on a plan that would have the offending players pay a $100 fine by May 1 to be eligible for Negro league play.[71] The fine applied to four of the Elites' stars: Wright, Glover, Byrd, and Gaines. Only Byrd and Gaines chose to pay it and return to Baltimore. In other decisions, the owners voted to introduce interleague play and to keep Wilson as league president.[72] With these matters settled, play began for the 1941 season.

The Elites started spring training in New Orleans on March 30, but not without more personnel changes. Wilson traded first baseman Red Moore, pitcher Tom Parker (who agreed to pay the $100 fine), and reserve catcher Everett Marshall to the Black Yankees for first baseman Johnny Washington. Washington was a gifted fielder, like Moore, but was a better hitter, finishing 1940 with a .343 average compared to Moore's .289.[73]

In another example of the league's loose operations and Wilson's inaction, Moore never reported to the Yankees, suffered no consequences, and the Yankees were left a player short from their trade with Baltimore. Moore headed home to Atlanta to take a job that gave him a draft deferment, a move that backfired on him. As he told the story in a 2006 interview:

I learned that if you had a job at the Post Office or railroad or something like that, they'd give you a deferment, so I called my daddy in Atlanta. He said, "Come on home, son, I'll get you a job." So I left the team to go home. He got me a job on the railroad, working 11 p.m. to 7 a.m. In about two weeks, a fella with more seniority took my job. I got a 3 p.m. to 11 p.m. job. My daddy asked me how I liked it and I told him I didn't 'cause I couldn't play ball, so he said, "Don't worry about it," and I quit. I knew there were ball teams in the City League set up by different companies. If you were a pretty good ball player, you'd have to work some, but they'd hire you. Some fellas saw me play and one of them worked at Colonial [Storage and Moving]. He was the manager of their team and he hired me. I got picked for the City League all-star team for a game against the Birmingham Black Barons. So, one day we were practicing in the schoolyard getting ready to play when I saw a big white fella standing over there; looked like a detective or something. He asked if I'd ever been in L.A. "Yeah," I told him. "I registered [for the draft] out there in 1940." [Moore had played with the Elites' entry in the California Winter League in 1940–41.] "We got business with you," he said. My number had come up and I didn't have any papers. With all the traveling I was doing, they never caught up with me. So this detective locked me up that evening. I had to get my mother and she had to get friends and relatives to testify at a trial that Atlanta, not Los Angeles, was my home. After they testified, the judge looked at me and said, "What would you rather do, go to the army or go to jail?" 'Course I chose the army.

Moore served in the army until 1945. He returned to Atlanta, where he worked at Colonial until he retired in 1981.[74]

With Moore's replacement, Washington, at first base, the Elites began two weeks of exhibition games against semipro teams, the Memphis Red Sox, and the St. Louis Stars. Then they met the Grays for two preseason games on Sunday, May 4th before 5,000 fans at Griffith Stadium. United States senator James Mead (R-NY) threw out the first ball while Washington Senators owner Clark Griffith looked on.[75]

Elites manager Snow gave Ace Adams the ball for game one. The Grays got to him for four runs in the first two innings on their way to a

9–6 win. The Elites bounced back to pull out game two by a score of 6–5, thanks to heroics by Scales and pitcher Bill Byrd, newly returned from Venezuela. With his back to the right-field wall, Scales leaped high to spear a line shot off the bat of Buck Leonard in the sixth inning to save two runs. Byrd, on his way to reestablishing himself as the staff ace, was called on to protect the one-run lead with no outs and two Grays on base in the ninth inning. He struck out the side.[76]

As they had done the year before, the two teams traveled to Harrisburg, Pennsylvania, for a final tune-up. One reporter described the game as "one of the wildest hitting games ever seen." Adams was again on the mound and again got clobbered as the Grays amassed fourteen hits and thirteen runs, while the Elites battered Grays pitchers Terris McDuffie and Ray Brown for eleven runs on fifteen hits. The Elites would have won had not Snow and Adams each made an error.[77]

The Elites and Grays opened the season on May 10 in Oriole Park in front of a crowd of 6,000. While the best the Elites could manage was a split, taking the first game 5–3 and losing the second 4–1, the afternoon produced bright omens for the season to come. Campanella hit a double to center and a two-run homer over the left field wall (though it was described as "baleful"), and Byrd pitched well in game one. Both would be major contributors in 1941.[78]

A setback the Elites took particularly hard was their 6–3 loss to the Cuban Stars in Yankee Stadium on Memorial Day. The game was the first Ruppert Cup game of the season. The gate receipts, which were substantial, as 20,000 people had come to see both the game and world heavyweight champion Joe Louis throw out the first ball, eased some of Wilson's pain over the loss.[79] The Elites then pulled off three wins in a row over the league-leading Cuban Stars on June 1–2 in Baltimore thanks in large part to the bat of Campanella, who had a league-leading .579 average.[80]

The Elites kept up the pace by winning six out of seven games behind the heavy hitting of Hoskins, Homer "Goose" Curry, and Charley Biot. Unfortunately, as well as the Elites played in May and June, the Grays played even better, taking first place in the first-half race.

As the second half got under way, the NAL and NNL teams played scheduled interleague games during the regular season for the first time. The Elites fared well at the expense of their NAL brethren. Byrd beat the Memphis Red Sox 3–2 by throwing eight innings of no-hit ball against them at Bugle Field on July 14.[81] The Kansas City Monarchs fell to the Elites 4–2 at Bugle Field in a night game on July 21 as Byrd won his sixth in a row; Snow, Campanella, and Pee Wee Butts chipped in with two hits apiece.[82] Fans showed their appreciation for Campanella's performance by electing him to the East team for the East-West classic. His fielding gems earned him the Most Valuable Player trophy. He nailed two runners trying to steal second, twice threw out the lead runner trying for second on sacrifice bunt attempts, and caught a foul ball in the stands.[83]

The Elites next met the Grays in Detroit's Briggs Stadium on Sunday, August 3, before 28,312 spectators. It was the first time in twenty years that Detroit Tigers owner Walter Briggs had allowed a Negro league game to be played there. The teams split a doubleheader. Jonas Gaines shut out the Grays, allowing only four scattered hits in game one, while his mates garnered nine hits and six runs. The Elites faltered in the nightcap 8–7.[84]

From Detroit, the team stopped in Kansas City for a Sunday doubleheader with the Monarchs on August 17. Future Hall of Fame Monarch pitcher Hilton Smith shut out the Elites 3–0 in game one. Monarchs pitcher Chet Brewer did not fare as well in game two, giving up nine hits and six runs to lose 6–4.[85] Four days later the Elites registered a 3–1 win over the St. Louis Stars in Hammond, Indiana. Jonas Gaines put in a record-breaking performance by striking out nineteen Stars to post his eighth win against only one loss. Campanella led the offense with a double and an inside-the-park home run achieved by driving the ball over center fielder Alfred "Buddy" Armour's head to the base of the center field fence, 410 feet away.[86]

The Elites again met the Grays for two doubleheaders nearer to home for both teams. The Grays bested the Elites 6–3 and 6–2 in Pittsburgh on August 23.[87] Then it was on to D.C. for a Sunday twin bill. For the first time in many years, the Grays would fail to finish above .500 in the second half of the season, in part because they lost both ends of this doubleheader to the Elites.[88]

Spotty recordkeeping led to alternate accounts of where the Elites finished in the second-half standings. The *Chicago Defender* credited the Elites with eleven league wins and five losses, good for second place.[89] Negro league historians Dick Clark and Larry Lester, on the other hand, put the Elites' second-half record at 9–8, good for third place.[90] Most importantly, however, both accounts agree that the Elites finished ahead of the Homestead Grays—only the second time the Elites had done so for either half of a season since coming to Baltimore.

The New York Cubans, who won the second-half pennant, lost the playoff to the Grays, giving the Grays one more Negro National League championship.[91]

Campanella's performance at the plate was a bright spot for the Elites in 1941. His defensive skills were always rated as among the best in the league, and this year his hitting drew rave reviews as well. He led the league in homers (32), doubles (24), and triples (14). He attracted the attention of Philadelphia Phillies scouts. The scouts asked him to practice with the team whenever he could and told him, "We may be able to sign you when something turns up." Campanella practiced with the Phillies every chance he got and also sought a tryout with Connie Mack's Philadelphia Athletics. Nothing "turned up" for Campanella with the Phillies or the A's.[92]

The Elites had acquitted themselves well during two years of disruptions to their roster brought about by trades and defections of star players to Latin America. They looked for better things in 1942.

For black Baltimoreans, Jim Crow remained alive and well. Mrs. Dorothy H. Hyde and Ms. Littie Mayor refused a Greyhound Bus driver's order to move to the back of the bus during a trip from Baltimore to New York City in September 1941. The driver put the women off the bus about 2:30 a.m. without their luggage or coats despite their pleas that it was cold. They waited at the edge of the highway until daybreak when a truck driver picked them up.[93] The NAACP protested the driver's action to the regional headquarters of the Pennsylvania Greyhound Lines. Regional manager J. Cummings promised to investigate and report back. No record of a report could be found.

As war raged in Europe, Baltimore's defense industries stepped up their production of war goods, including steel. Baltimore's steel industry hired record numbers of workers. Ministers and prominent NAACP lawyers, including Thurgood Marshall, urged black citizens to sign up for unions, some of which were willing to work mixed crews.[94] Through meetings with Maryland governor Herbert R. O'Conor (D, 1939–47), the Baltimore chapter of the Congress of Industrial Organizations (CIO) succeeded in persuading certain manufacturing companies, such as Celanese and Kelly Springfield, to hire some black workers.[95]

Jim Crow still reigned, but he would start losing his grip as the war effort intensified.

CHAPTER 3

War on the Home Front

Elites Nail Another Pennant

World War II had engulfed the European and Pacific theaters as the 1942 season opened. Major League Baseball commissioner Kenesaw "Mountain" Landis, in a letter to President Roosevelt, questioned whether baseball should continue in the midst of a world war. Roosevelt replied with what has become known as the Green Light letter, saying he thought baseball should continue, as it would be a needed morale booster.[1] By implication, Negro league baseball also had Roosevelt's blessings to continue.

The city was in the midst of an employment boom, which helped ease racial tensions by putting large numbers of blacks and whites to work. During the boom, Baltimore gained 215,000 jobs while losing 55,000 employees to military service. Approximately 40,000 of the jobs created between April 1940 and November 1943 went to blacks, many of whom had been unemployed.[2] Most were low-paying jobs like manufacturing fifty-five-gallon drums, bagging fertilizer, and handling heavy machinery,[3] but the increase in jobs brought more fans to Bugle Field.

The Elites started well in 1942. Four of the team's stars who had jumped their contracts and gone to Mexico for the 1941 season returned home—"Wild Bill" Wright, the Mexican Leagues' leading hitter in '41; second baseman Sammy T. Hughes; and pitchers Andy Porter and Tom Glover. In addition, center fielder Henry Kimbro returned from his one-year stay with the Black Yankees. The Elites' 1939 outfield of Wright, Kimbro, and Hoskins—considered the best in the league—was reunited. Only two members of the '41 Elites would not be on board for 1942: Johnny Washington was the first Elite to be drafted, and Wilson had released "Goose" Curry to the Philadelphia Stars, only because they had offered Curry the manager's job.[4]

The reconstituted Elites began their 1942 campaign in Philadelphia's Parkside Field against the Stars. As much as Curry wanted to beat his former mates before his new home crowd, the Stars lost the opener to the Elites 2–1. Curry settled for driving former Elite first baseman Jim West home for the Stars' only run. Ace Adams went the distance for the Elites, yielding only five hits. Curry lost another squeaker the next day, May 10, in ten innings as the Elites opened their home season in Oriole Park with a doubleheader before 5,500 fans who saw six homers in game one. Campanella, Hughes, and Kimbro connected for the Elites, but it was Campanella's single, driving Hughes home, that won the game.

Local celebrity "Little Willie" Adams, along with Kenneth Bass and Askew Gatewood, two fellow "sportsmen," a term used by reporters to denote numbers bosses, combined to execute the first pitch ceremony. One took the role of pitcher, another the role of catcher, and the third stepped up to the plate, bat in hand, to swing at the offering. The result of the swing seems not to have been recorded.[5]

Umpires called the second game in the third inning due to the 6:00 p.m. curfew, so Wright's first homer since his return went for naught.[6] A fight between fans after the game was called resulted in minor damage to the park. It was enough, however, for the owners to disallow any more Negro league games in Oriole Park, forcing the Elites to play all the remaining 1942 home games at the smaller Bugle Field.[7] The good news was that the Elites were off to a 2–0 start. The next league test was a doubleheader with the Grays the next Sunday in Griffith Stadium.

The Elites entered Griffith Stadium two games behind the Grays. They took a 5–4 lead into the bottom of the ninth of game one, only to have the Grays push across a run on a sacrifice fly by Lick Carlisle to tie the game. Campanella came through once again with a tenth-inning, game-winning single to drive in Bill Hoskins, who had tripled

All-Star Elites'
center fielder
Henry "Kimmie" Kimbro

off the right field wall. Game two was another close one, but the Grays prevailed this time, 3–2. Josh Gibson, returned from Venezuela, was in midseason form for the Grays, going 3 for 6 on the day including a triple and a homer.[8]

The Elites continued to play well, and two wins in early July sealed the first-half pennant for them. They bested the Grays 1–0 on Thursday night, July 2, at Bugle Field behind the four-hit pitching of Jonas Gaines. Before 12,000 fans at Yankee Stadium on July 4, Byrd and Porter combined their talents on the mound to beat the Eagles 8–4. Campanella connected for a double and two singles.[9]

In the eighth inning, Byrd's fastball struck Newark's shortstop Willie

Wells on his temple. Wells fell to the ground unconscious and had to be carried from the field. He came to in the dressing room.[10] Some claim that Wells's beaning that day prompted him to invent the first modern-day baseball helmet, cut down from a construction worker's hard hat.[11] Wells did invent the modern-day batting helmet, but not because of this incident. He had worn a helmet during a game in Buffalo in 1939; what prompted him to do so is not known.[12]

The Elites got off to a good start in the second half. In mid-July they split a Sunday doubleheader at Bugle Field with the Black Yankees to keep a three-game lead over the Grays. Player-manager Felton Snow provided fireworks in the nightcap by taking a swing at umpire Fred McCrary over a disputed called third strike. Police officers escorted Snow from the field. Wilson, as NNL president, in a rare exercise of authority, suspended his own manager for three games and fined him $25.[13]

The Newark Eagles dealt the Elites a setback later in the month, on the 24th, when Leon Day fanned eighteen Elites, keeping them to one hit, in an 8–1 Eagle victory at Bugle Field. The loss put a stop to the Elites' seven-game winning streak that had led the league.[14] The Negro League Baseball Players Association credits Day with the league record for strikeouts in a single game for the eighteen he threw that day.[15] That distinction actually belongs to Elites pitcher Jonas Gaines, who had struck out nineteen St. Louis Stars a year earlier in Hammond, Indiana.

As Labor Day approached, the Elites were only a half-game behind the Grays but were now without the services of Campanella, who had jumped to Mexico.[16] The Elites closed out their home season on Sunday, September 6, in, as one observer described it, "a mingled picture of glory and despair" as they divided a doubleheader with the Philadelphia Stars.[17]

The Elites had to sweep the Labor Day September 7th doubleheader in Philadelphia to beat out the Grays for the second-half flag. The Elites captured the opener 6–0 behind Bill Harvey's three-hit masterpiece and with timely hits from Kimbro, Butts, and Hoskins. The Stars put an end to the Elites' pennant hopes by beating them 4–3 in game two. Curry scored the winning run.[18]

Long-time Elites third baseman and manager Felton Snow

How the Grays advanced to the Negro League World Series to face the Kansas City Monarchs, winners of the Negro American League pennant is a Negro leagues decision-making mystery not unlike the four-team playoffs of 1939. No record of a playoff between the Elites, who had won the first-half flag, and the Grays, who won the second-half pennant, can be found. The Grays and the Kansas City Monarchs played the first game of the World Series in Griffith Stadium on September 8th.[19]

The Elites hooked up with the crosstown Baltimore Orioles for a

Souvenir stadium pin circa 1942. Fans bought the pins at the ballpark and pinned them to their clothing.

series of postseason exhibition games in Oriole Park. Many of the white fans, referred to as "closet Confederates" by author Charles Osgood, who attended one of the games with his father as guests of Orioles manager Tommy Thompson, held the Elites in low esteem. They saw the Elites as more of a group of railroad porters playing out of their league than as professional baseball players. When young Charles asked his father why the Elites were not playing in the minors and majors, Osgood Sr. replied, "Well, Charlie, they're flashy alright but they're not steady enough to play the whole season." Osgood Jr. calls his father's answer "not one to be bronzed."[20]

Notable Opening Day Dignitaries

Players "had to be there two hours ahead of game time," said Philadelphia Stars catcher Stanley Glenn of opening day, "to sign autographs, pose for pictures. Whatever the fans wanted you to do, that's what you did. All the high schools were there with their drum and bugle corps and all those little girls with those little dresses on. And of course, politicians would always be there."[21]

The majors and the Negro leagues shared the opening day tradition of inviting a dignitary, usually a politician, to throw out the first ball. Ever since President Taft had thrown out a ceremonial ball to start a game on April 14, 1910, at Griffith Stadium, the Senators' owner had invited the nation's chief executive to start the major league season by throwing a ball on opening day to a waiting Washington Senators catcher surrounded by the press corps.[22]

The Negro leagues never attracted the president to an opening day game, but it was not for lack of trying. Tom Wilson invited Franklin Roosevelt to throw out the first ball of the Washington Elites' 1936 season in Griffith Stadium but received a reply that FDR was too busy.[23] Roosevelt was, however, at Griffith Stadium to start the Washington Senators' 1936 season, as he was for every opening day for the first eight years of his presidency.[24] In FDR's absence, Senator Sherman Minton (D-IN), future Supreme Court justice and staunch supporter of Roosevelt, who may have recommended him to Wilson, did the honors to open the Elites' 1936 season, at Griffith Stadium on May 16 in a game against the Newark Eagles.[25] Minton did the honors again to start the 1937 season at Griffith Stadium.[26]

The most notable opening day ball tossers at Bugle Field were Marse S. Callaway, William L. "Little Willie" Adams, and Mayor Theodore R. McKeldin.[27] All were significant figures for Baltimore's black community. Callaway, a leading black politician and businessman, ran a successful real estate business, Marse S. Callaway, Inc., from offices at 2128 Madison Avenue in Old West. His slogan was, "It's Easy to Own Your Own Home."[28] Callaway moved to Baltimore in 1917 and in 1918 married Julia Lawson, an organist at John Wesley Methodist Church. Active in

Opening Day broadside

Republican politics from the early 1920s until his death in 1959, Callaway served as an investigator for the Liquor Board and was a member of the Commission on Scholarships for Negroes. He founded the first police school for black applicants at the Bethel A.M.E. church in 1937. Callaway formed the Colored Republican Voters League and served as an alternate delegate to the Republican National Convention from Maryland in 1944 and 1948. His political column, "Behind the Scenes," regularly appeared in the *Afro-American*. At Callaway's funeral, on May 23, 1959, Governor McKeldin (R, 1951–59), U.S. senator J. Glenn Beall (R-MD, 1953–65), five ministers, seven lay officiants, and a large vested choir took three hours to pay tribute to Callaway at the Sharon Baptist Church, where he had been a long-time member. The funeral rites were conducted with "pomp never before accorded a Negro political figure in this city."[29]

The biggest African American entrepreneurial success story in Baltimore belonged to William "Little Willie" Adams. He got his nickname from an associate who thought Adams resembled a main underworld character, played by Edward G. Robinson, in the 1930 movie *Little Cae-*

sar. In a literal rags to riches story, Adams began his career with a $6-a-week job in an East Baltimore rag packing plant. He found better work at a bicycle repair shop, where he met men who made a lot of money running numbers in the city's thriving illegal gambling business. Adams soon became the most successful numbers man in the city.[30] Running numbers was not without its dangers, as Adams discovered on June 18, 1938, when a bomb went off in the three-story building in Old West, at Druid Hill Avenue and Whitelock Street, that housed Little Willie's Tavern and his luxurious apartment. Police speculated that the bombing was related to a feud between rival numbers factions.[31] In the late 1940s he reduced his numbers work so he could give more attention to other interests. Adams joined with Henry Parks to form the Parks Sausage Company. Many Baltimoreans remember the company's advertising slogan, "More Parks sausages, Mom, please!" Parks Sausage became one of the largest black-owned firms in America. The two men would eventually sell it for five million dollars. By 1979, Adams had interests in apartment buildings, liquor stores, rental properties, shopping centers, a senior citizens' housing project in Forest Park, and a low-income housing project in Philadelphia.[32]

"For all his wealth and fame," Old West entrepreneur Clarence Brown said of Adams, "you'd never know he was a millionaire. He had no expensive car. He hung out with folks like me. His office was in the 1500 block of Pennsylvania Avenue. He'd park his car on Mosher Street and walk around the corner to his office. If somebody'd ask him for a dollar or forty cents, he'd say, 'come up to my office.'"[33]

Adams survived several criminal investigations, including one by the U.S. Senate's Kefauver Committee on organized crime, to whom he admitted making $1,000 a week from numbers. The U.S. Supreme Court overturned a conviction he received for violating state lottery laws. In 1979 Adams attributed his legal problems to the fact that "I was the first black man in this city who could afford to move into a well-off white suburban community." He and Victorine were the only black residents on Carlisle Avenue,[34] farther out on the west side of town than blacks had previously ventured.

To many whites, Adams appeared to be a shadowy criminal boss with underworld ties. Most blacks regarded him as a Horatio Alger figure who had parlayed his street smarts into fame, fortune, and respectability. He was the commencement speaker at Morris Brown College in Atlanta, Georgia, in May of 1977 and received an honorary doctorate.[35]

Everyone in the black community knew how he made his money, and many admired him for the same reason they admired two other Old West black businessmen, Melvin Williams and Clinton "Shorty" Bruise. Williams and Bruise sold fruits and vegetables from wagons drawn by ponies stabled behind the York Hotel. *Afro-American* columnist Early Byrd explained: "What we had in common is that we all wanted to be independent of a racist white society. That's why we admired men like 'Little Willie.'"[36]

Theodore McKeldin advocated equal treatment for blacks, first as Republican mayor of Baltimore (1943–47), later as governor of Maryland (1951–59), and again during his second tenure as mayor (1963–67). He left no doubt about his commitment to improving housing conditions for blacks. In his first mayoral inaugural address, on May 18, 1943, he said: "It is unintelligent and shocking that the shelter of a large element of our population, contributing importantly to the economic life of the community, should be left so utterly neglected. . . . Not colored people alone are affected when crowded, unsanitary conditions are allowed to persist. . . . Disease germs respect no barrier of race or creed or social conditions."[37]

Ronald A. Rooks, black and an art and antiques appraiser, remembered McKeldin as "black-oriented, . . . out of fifty-two weeks every year he'd spend forty Sundays at black churches. Sometimes he'd speak. Sometimes he'd just sit there. He was always late," Rooks added, "because in those days mayors had so many other things to do."[38]

McKeldin did more for blacks in Baltimore than attend their church services. In response to a June 1943 letter from Randall L. Tyrus, executive director of the Baltimore branch of the NAACP expressing concern that "Baltimore escape the tragic incidents [race riots] such as occurred in Detroit, Mobile, and Beaumont [Texas]," McKeldin wrote back three days later saying, "to help avoid similar outbreaks in our City you may depend upon me for whatever cooperation is needed. On my own ini-

Mayor Theodore R. McKeldin

tiative I have already made some inquiries and made some suggestions with reference to this matter."[39] McKeldin appointed the first African American to the school board and to the solicitor's office. He established the first summer camp for black children.[40] McKeldin established the Advisory Committee on City Housing in May 1945 to "find practical relief as a social necessity and soften . . . increased pressure and demand for adequate Baltimore housing." The mayor appointed the police commissioner, health commissioner, chief engineer, and the director of the Baltimore Housing Authority to the committee.[41]

His initiatives did not sit well with some whites. One Victor E. Schminke wrote to him objecting to McKeldin's "thrusting your Republican pro-negro policies upon us—the latest being another bi-racial commission." After recounting "the outrages perpetrated against the whites—especially white women," Schminke concluded that "enforcement of the Jim Crow laws, more white police—will do more—negro psychology being what it is—to promote—to induce—orderly—and ultimately—amicable—racial relations,—than all the pro-negro bi-racial commissions."[42]

McKeldin did not flinch. Addison V. Pinkney, executive secretary of the Baltimore NAACP wrote to him in July 1945, "We have just learned of your fearless and courageous stand before the Fulton Improvement Association. . . . We believe that your attitude is in keeping with the principles of true democracy . . . and stands out as an indication of an upward trend in government for *all the people* in Baltimore."[43]

Muddling Through

Employment for both whites and blacks remained at an all-time high in 1943, even as discrimination remained in force. When challenged, many white organizations pointed to the custom of discrimination as the way things were done. White crane operators, for instance, brought work to a halt in November 1943 at the Bethlehem-Fairfield shipyards and forced 30,000 employees to lose a day's work to protest an attempt to gain permission for African Americans to operate cranes. A company spokesman claimed, "Colored employees are barred from jobs of crane operators."[44] Commander Howard A. Kelly Jr., commanding officer of the Coast Guard Port Security Regiment and a son of famous Baltimore physician Howard A. Kelly Sr., first professor of gynecology at the Johns Hopkins Medical School, turned down three blacks who tried to enlist in the regiment in November of 1943. Commander Kelly explained that a colored unit would not be organized because they would have to guard piers in the harbor and that meant colored members would be giving orders to white stevedores. "This wouldn't work in Baltimore," he said.[45] In the fall of 1943, an independent union, the Point Breeze Employees Association (PBEA) threatened to strike the Western Electric Company unless separate toilets were made available for the black employees being hired. The company had put business ahead of custom. A spokesman said that constructing separate facilities would take time and labor away from production and that the constant transfer of employees among departments would make separate facilities impractical. Charles H. Dorn, representing PBEA, countered that, while the city's plumbing code made separate facilities unnecessary "discrimination is the custom here."[46]

Even the city-financed Enoch Pratt Free Library denied Miss Louise Kerr, a teacher from Baltimore's colored public school system, admittance to a training course for aspiring librarians in 1943.[47] Library trustees, while hiring only white employees, allowed blacks to use the library because its founder, Enoch Pratt, had so stipulated in 1884 when he turned over control of the library system to the city. Pratt said at the time that it was his wish that the libraries be "accessible for all, rich and poor, without distinction of race or color."[48]

The Elites remained caught in the web of discrimination as the owners of Oriole Park continued the ban of the team from its confines that had begun in May 1942. Wilson and Green also faced challenges brought on by the draft, gasoline restrictions, the bounty of wartime jobs that attracted players, and the deep pockets of the Mexican League. This year the tinkling of pesos drew the Elite Giants trio of Wright, Campanella, and Butts to Mexico.

Wilson sent three replacements from his Nashville Cubs—Harvey Young to replace Butts, Frank "Junior" Russell to take over at third if Snow, whom Wilson had replaced as manager with George Scales, did not return, and a second baseman, also named George Scales but no relation to the manager. Clarence James, a Baltimore native, and "Dink" Canada, a hefty first baseman from Birmingham, Alabama, rounded out the newcomers to the Elites' spring training camp.[49] Canada and newcomer Scales did not make the team.[50]

The Elites held spring training in Baltimore and conducted a shortened preseason game schedule due to restrictions on the use of gasoline. The Office of Defense Transportation (ODT) restricted all teams' travel options in 1943 by banning the use of gasoline for driving for recreational purposes. Joseph P. Eastman, of the ODT, interpreted the ban to preclude the use of team buses for baseball games, be the teams white or black. His ruling meant that teams would have to travel by rail, regular bus services, or private cars; each was a more expensive option than a team bus. Sportswriter Art Carter described Eastman's ruling as a "death blow" for Negro league teams. Officials in both leagues considered halting play for the season. Negro National League team owners, whose cities were closer together than were the Negro American League teams', decided at their April meeting at the Columbia Lodge Elks Home in Washington, D.C., to carry on, albeit with a reduced schedule. Negro American League owners were undecided at the April meeting but later decided also to play a reduced schedule of games.[51]

The lure of well-paying defense jobs enticed Vic Harris, player-manager of the Washington-Homestead Grays, to retire from baseball for two years to work full-time in Pittsburgh, though he was available to play on weekends.[52] "Biz" Mackey, now with the Newark Eagles, stayed home in Los Angeles for both the 1942 and 1943 seasons for the same reason.[53] Four Elites—Hoskins, Kimbro, Glover, and Harvey—considered foregoing baseball for the defense jobs that they had started over the winter.[54] Fortunately for the Elites, they decided on baseball and reported to spring training.

The 1943 season's festivities began at Griffith Stadium on May 16 with the usual Sunday doubleheader. The Grays had edged the Elites for the pennant the previous three years and there was no reason to think the same two teams would not battle each other for the pennant this year. The Elites arrived in D.C. with some new faces. Veteran pitchers Byrd, Glover, and Harvey were still on board. They were supplemented by two lefties, Bill Burns, obtained from the Black Yankees, and James Carter from New Auburn, Indiana. Robert Clarke took Campanella's place behind the plate, Felton Snow returned to play third, the newcomers Russell and Young held down second and short, while manager Scales was at first. "Biggie" Williams, from the Baltimore-based semipro Edgewater Elites, replaced Wright in right field, and veterans Kimbro and Hoskins completed the outfield.[55]

Congressman William L. Dawson, a Democrat from Chicago and the only Negro member of Congress, threw out the first ball. Judge Armond W. Scott of Washington raised the flag in center field. Washington Senators owner Clark Griffith and U.S. senator James Mead were again among the 8,000 fans on hand for the NNL's season opener.

The Elites dropped both games to the Grays, 2–1 and 7–0. Josh Gibson weighed in with a five-for-six day, including four doubles. The Grays overran the Elites again the next day in Portsmouth, Virginia, 8–3. The two teams played to a 5–5 tie in Portsmouth two days later. In their first appearance at Yankee Stadium, on Sunday, May 23, Wilson's men dropped a doubleheader to the New York Cubans, 9–2 and 10–3.[56]

The Elites did not play a game at Bugle Field until May 30 when they met the Grays for a twin bill. Newly elected Mayor McKeldin was late for his first ball-tossing assignment.[57] He arrived at the game with Marse Callaway and gave a five-minute speech to the assembled fans.[58] The two men may have inspired the team, for the Elites, badly in need of a win, took the Grays' measure twice, 11–8 and 2–0.[59]

The Elites won only two games during the first two weeks of June. By the 19th, their record stood at 4–11, putting them in sixth place in the now seven-team league while the Grays held down first place. (A St. Louis–Harrisburg club had joined the league.) So stood the two teams when the first half ended. Through the second half of the season, the Elites won a game here and there except when they faced the Grays. In a Sunday doubleheader at Griffith Stadium on August 22, the Grays ganged up on Elites pitchers Manuel Stewart, Porter, Burns, Harvey, and Mike Berry for 39 hits and 33 runs to overwhelm the Elites 19–3 and 14–4. Perhaps the Elites were exhausted. They had dropped a doubleheader to the Grays the day before in Pittsburgh, 9–1 and 4–1. Gibson launched four homers over the weekend.[60] The Elites ended the second half in fifth place out of six teams. (The St. Louis–Harrisburg team folded.) The Grays again won the National League pennant.

The 1943 season had been a disappointing one for the Elite Giants. They suffered from the absence of Wright, Campanella, and Butts and the impact of the draft, which was about to further damage the line-up. Second baseman Sammy T. Hughes and pitchers Jonas Gaines, Bill Burns, Bill Harvey, and Joe Black traded baseball uniforms for Uncle Sam's when the 1943 season ended.[61]

Fortunately for the Elites, Joe Black, who would develop into a star pitcher, was given nearby stateside duty and was available to pitch on occasional weekends. Black had joined the Elites in 1943 as a shortstop, but George Scales, in his role as manager, called the young man aside and told him, "You're too lazy to be a shortstop but you can throw hard. I'm gonna try you as a pitcher." In his first start, Black fanned the first seven batters he faced, but the eighth batter ignited an eight-run barrage against him. "So," Black recounted later, "I decided I ought to learn how to pitch, and laid out of school a year to do nothing but play ball."[62] He returned to his studies after his pitching improved, graduating from Baltimore's Morgan State College (now University) in 1950.[63]

Scales had well-deserved reputations for developing players and for having a temper. Ted Page, a pitcher, remembered Scales's berating Josh Gibson in the showers in 1931, when all three played for the Grays, for dropping a foul ball. Resenting Scales's tone of voice, "George and I tangled up," Page said. "Buck naked, I knocked George's tooth out." Another Gray, George Britt, separated Scales and Page, but moments later, Page said, "George charged me again under the shower. He had a knife and cut me in the belly." Britt separated them again, this time with the help of Jud Wilson. That night, Page and Scales, who were roommates and had been friends before the fight, slept, as usual, in one bed. "George slept facing that way," Page said, "I slept facing this way. George had his knife under the pillow and I always carried a pistol . . . We didn't get a wink of sleep that night." They patched up their differences by throwing a party for the team in their room the next night.[64]

Butts remembered Scales as "a hot boiler." "Scales was a little hard on you, but if you'd listen, you could learn a lot." Scales convinced Butts to give up swinging for the fences by saying, " 'the more you swing the less you hit the ball. Just get on base, walk, anything.' Sure enough," Butts said, "he stopped me right there. He cooled me on that . . . He was watching everything."[65]

Byrd, whom Campanella referred to as "Daddy" because of Byrd's

First baseman and manager George Scales

concern for younger players, also offered advice to players on many top-ics. He once counseled Joe Black in the language of ballplayers by saying, "You have a chance to be a good pitcher, but don't let your fastball leave through the head of your pecker."[66] Byrd said about his coaching, "We didn't have coaches in those days. The young fellows needed help. It was up to us older fellows to teach them how to play."[67]

The Elites, looking to make some postseason money, engaged a team of minor league all-stars, the International All-Stars, for postseason exhibition play at Bugle Field. The Elites compiled a 6–1 record against the All-Stars in a welcome break from their record in the regular season. The first game was described as "sweet revenge" for the Elites. They defeated former Oriole pitcher Don Kerr, who had bested them in an exhibition game earlier in the season when Kerr was pitching for the Curtis Bay Coast Guard team.[68]

The Elites' final 1943 performance at Bugle Field was a doubleheader against a team of major and minor leaguers brought together by Washington Senators scout and former Bugle Field owner Joe Cambria. Seven

Washington Senators were on Cambria's multileague roster, including Mickey Vernon, Early Wynn, and Sherry Robertson. True to their 1943 form, the Elites dropped both games, 10–1 and 4–1.[69]

When the Elites returned to action in 1944, the war had turned in the Allies' favor, even though London had been damaged by an onslaught of German bombing runs. The Allied Forces took Rome, invaded Normandy, and liberated Paris. General MacArthur returned to the Philippines as he'd promised and liberated the islands from the Japanese. The Germans lost the Battle of the Bulge.[70]

At home, Baltimore's Lyric Theater continued its custom of barring African American performers from its stage. Frederick Huber, managing director of the theater, said in early March that the Lyric was unavailable for the dates Eleanor Roosevelt, wife of Franklin Roosevelt, and black musician Duke Ellington, wanted to rent it. Huber also turned away the National Maritime Union (CIO), which planned a ceremony to honor merchant seamen. Paul Robeson, the black star of *Othello* on Broadway, had agreed to sing at the ceremony. Two months earlier, the theater had barred vocalist Anne W. Brown, original cast star of *Porgy and Bess*. Ms. Brown sang at the Enon Baptist Church instead.[71]

Louise Kerr, the teacher who wanted to take a library training course, subsequently applied for a job at the library. The library refused her application. She then sued the Pratt Library trustees, who successfully argued that the Fourteenth Amendment, providing for equal protection for all, did not require the library to consider her application.[72] On March 7, Judge W. Calvin Chestnut dismissed Kerr's suit in federal court by ruling that the library was a private, not a governmental, agency and that the trustees' practice of hiring only white staff was not done out of prejudice but was based on the fact that most patrons were white and would be best served by white staff.[73]

Mayor McKeldin notched a victory against discrimination when he appointed black, Yale-educated attorney George W. F. McMechen to be the city's first African American member of the school board.[74]

Gas rationing remained in effect, but the ODT lifted the ban on pleasure driving, allowing the Elites to take the team bus when they went south to Little Rock, Arkansas, for spring training. Wilson put

Felton Snow back in the skipper's job, while Scales stayed with the team as a player. Campanella and Butts returned from Mexico.[75] Wilson and Campanella patched up their disagreement to the point that Wilson forgave the fine and offered Campanella $3,000 for the 1944 season and promised it for the 1945 season plus $300 more each season if the team did well. Campanella accepted.[76] Butts anchored the infield at shortstop. An early report had a lanky Puerto Rican named Leonardo Chapman at first base. He ended up with the Indianapolis Clowns. Scales, Snow, Wesley "Doc" Dennis, and Frank Russell, from Nashville's sandlots, alternated at first, second, and third. Hoskins and Kimbro were ready for duty in the outfield. Norman "Bobby" Robinson held down the third outfield spot in the absence of Wright, who was still in Mexico. Porter, Byrd, Glover, and Harvey returned to pitch.[77]

The Elites' 1944 exhibition games received little coverage. They opened the season in front of their Bugle Field fans on Sunday, May 7th. McKeldin was again on hand to start the game. He chose a three-man act to open the season, much as Adams had two years earlier, but McKeldin racially integrated his act. Fans saw the white mayor on the mound look for his signal from a black businessman behind the plate, Marse Callaway. White police commissioner H. R. Atkinson stepped into the batter's box and lined the mayor's offering into center field.[78] McKeldin had dealings with both men off the field. He met regularly with Callaway. The mayor's appointment books from 1943 to 1947 reveal numerous scheduled meetings with Callaway and show Callaway's private telephone number, MA 6319, in the books' directory section.[79] McKeldin would appoint Atkinson to a housing commission in 1945.

The mayor may have again inspired the Elites, for they played well that day. They beat the Philadelphia Stars 15–5 and 9–0 before a capacity crowd of 7,000 fans. The Elites' twenty-nine hits over the course of both games avenged their 5–4 loss to the Stars the day before in Philadelphia. Glover held the Stars to three hits en route to a shut-out in game two.[80]

But, as had happened the year before following McKeldin's appearance at opening day, the Elites then went into a slump. During the week of May 18 they dropped three out of four to the Grays at Bugle Field[81]

The 1944 Baltimore Elite Giants. Standing, left to right: *Roy Campanella, Lester Lockett, Donald Troy, Thomas Glover, Laymon Yokeley, Wesley Dennis, Bill Hoskins, and Andrew Porter.* Kneeling, left to right: *identity uncertain, Felton Snow, Bill Harvey, Henry Kimbro, Norman Robinson, Tom Butts, Frank Russell, and George Scales.*

and narrowly lost both ends of a doubleheader in Griffith Stadium to the Poseymen on Sunday, May 28. Sportswriter Sam Lacy called those two games "the best played in [Washington] in the history of league baseball. They were marked by air-tight pitching, brilliant fielding, and timely hitting. The crowd of 8,000 left fully satisfied."[82]

The Elites managed to pick up their pace in June. They took three of four games from the Eagles at Bugle Field, split a Yankee Stadium doubleheader with the Cubans, and beat the Grays two out of three at home.[83] Still, when the first half of the season ended, the Elites were in their familiar runner-up spot behind the Grays.

An event upsetting to Baltimore's baseball fans then occurred. Oriole Park burned to the ground in the late evening and early morning hours of July 3–4. Rumors sprang up that the Orioles would displace the Elites from Bugle Field. McKeldin squelched the rumors by arranging for the Orioles to play at Municipal Stadium, near 33rd Street and Greenmount Avenue, leaving Bugle Field to the Elites. Municipal Stadium had previously been used only for football. In recounting how he made the offer to the O's, McKeldin said, "I was at Oriole Park the morning it burned down and offered the facilities of the Baltimore [Municipal] Stadium to Tommy Thomas, the manager of the baseball club. He accepted the offer."[84]

Assured of their tenure in Bugle Field, the Elites got off to a strong start in the second half by beating the Eagles in back-to-back games in Harrisburg and at Bugle Field 4–2 and 11–6 on July 10th and 11th.[85] They took three straight from the New York Black Yankees at Bugle Field July 21–23.[86]

As July turned to August, the Elites' fortunes faded. When the second-half dust settled after a Labor Day doubleheader at Ruppert Stadium with the Eagles, which the teams split, the Elites, at 15–10, were in third place behind the 15–7 Stars and the pennant-winning Grays at 12–5.[87] The Elites' disappointing performance on the field was not accompanied by a drop in ticket sales. The predictions that a wartime economy would bode well for baseball continued to hold, as attested to by the 14,000 fans who witnessed the doubleheader.[88]

The fighting in Europe ended in the spring of 1945, and GI's began returning home, among them a number of Negro leaguers ready to resume their baseball careers. Jonas Gaines rejoined the Elites from the army toward the end of the 1945 season. In October of that year, Branch Rickey, general manager of the major league Brooklyn Dodgers, announced the biggest baseball news in fifty years—that he had signed Kansas City Monarch infielder Jackie Robinson to a contract with the Dodgers organization as a Montreal Royal. Rickey's action put the first crack in the major leagues' color bar.

Some cracks could be seen in Baltimore's color bar as well. Seventeen of twenty-eight stores surveyed by the *Afro-American* offered equal service to all shoppers, although the remaining eleven, which included some of the city's largest stores, such as Hutzler's and Hochschild's, did not.[89] The Fourth United States Circuit Court of Appeals, in a decision written by Judge Morris A. Soper of Baltimore on April 17, reversed Judge Chestnut's decision and ruled that the Pratt Library was a public institution and, as such, subject to the provisions of the Fourteenth Amendment. The Appeals Court also ruled, "There can be no doubt that the applicant [Kerr] was excluded from the school because of her race." Library trustees initially accepted the Appeals Court ruling but changed their minds a week later and filed an appeal with the Supreme Court on the advice of their lawyer, Harry N. Baetjer. The high court declined to hear the case.[90]

McKeldin continued his campaign against discrimination by leading a group of city officials on a tour to the 1300 block of Gilmore and the 600 block of Pierce Streets, both within Old West. There the groups saw unsanitary outhouses, broken wooden fences, and houses without a back wall in which people still lived. McKeldin used the tour to bring pressure on building inspectors and landlords to put the city's housing in proper repair. Too often it would take a year and a half for a violation complaint to make it to court, where, frequently, the judge let the landlord off with a small fine.[91]

Elsewhere it was business as usual. The state-operated ferries conveying passengers across the Chesapeake Bay maintained separate sections on deck for "white" and "colored" as indicated by signs with letters two inches high.[92] The Governor's Commission on Problems Affecting Colored People, a biracial group appointed by Governor O'Conor four years earlier, frequently could not attract a quorum to its meetings. When a quorum was achieved, lengthy discussions usually ended in a stalemate, with whites on one side of the issue and blacks on the other side.[93]

The Elites set up spring training for the 1945 season at Ponce de Leon Park in Atlanta at the end of March. Wild Bill Wright returned from Mexico. Felton Snow remained as the manager. Wilson traded former Elites manager George Scales back to the Black Yankees once again, this time for second baseman Harry Williams. Roland "Archie" Hinton, a rookie from Los Angeles, made a good impression as a promising pitcher and infielder.[94]

In their season opener at Bugle Field on May 6th, the Elites split a Sunday doubleheader with the Philadelphia Stars 6–2 and 5–8 before a full house of 6,000 fans. A pinch-hit homer by Bill Byrd in the ninth inning won game one.[95] McKeldin and Callaway were again on hand to get the season started. Callaway swung on and missed the mayor's offering from the mound.[96] The name of the catcher at this year's opening ceremonies was not reported. The Elites won all of their league games during the rest of May but again stumbled in June. With the Grays, they traveled to Detroit on June 7th to play one of the few Negro league games that Tigers owner Walter Briggs allowed in Briggs Stadium that year. The Elites did not score a run all day. The Grays shut them out 1–0 and 5–0. Byrd and Roy Welmaker hooked up in a pitcher's duel in game one until the ninth, when Leonard singled, Gibson doubled, Sam Bankhead walked, and Vic Harris brought Leonard home on a sacrifice fly. A 365-foot drive by Gibson into the left field bleachers led the Grays' attack in game two. The double loss dropped the Elites into fourth place.[97] The Grays, to no one's surprise, went on to win the first-half pennant.

As the second half of the season got under way, Fay Young, *Chicago Defender* sportswriter, called attention to the increasing number of disturbances in the stands. In an article, Young asked fans and players to behave themselves and the police to make more arrests, lest Negro league baseball "be broken up by the rowdies who seek to break up or destroy everything in sight." Incidents cited by Young included two players going after an umpire, which resulted in the management of Wrigley Field canceling four scheduled doubleheaders; five fights among fans in Comiskey Park; ten fights stopped by the police in Detroit's Briggs Stadium during a Sunday doubleheader; and a fan's stealing a deputy sheriff's gun at Red Bird Stadium in Columbus, Ohio, and shooting three people, fortunately none fatally. The Red Bird Stadium management responded by barring Negro teams from the park, but later relented.[98]

Most of the fights were between men, but black sportswriter Dan Burley noted that women sometimes also took part. "Black women,"

The 1945 Baltimore Elite Giants. Standing, left to right: *Andy Porter, Tom Glover, Bill Hoskins, unidentified, Harry Williams, Frank Duncan III, Bill Byrd, Wesley Dennis, and Donald Troy.* Kneeling, left to right: *Roy Campanella, Robert Clarke, Tom Walker, Norman Robinson, Henry Kimbro, Roland Hinton, and Felton Snow.*

Burley wrote, "can fight like cats and dogs over the affections of some slick-headed playboy." If upset enough, he said, a black woman could "rise up and start pounding her man over the head with her purse, with lurid, vulgar curses pouring from her lips."[99]

The Elites fared better in the second half. They took the pennant fight with the Grays to the last game of the season. In the midst of their success, Tom Glover, who had won five games in ten starts, jumped the Elites to play in Mexico, saying that he was dissatisfied with his role on the team. Manager Snow and co-owner Green issued the usual threat that Glover would be subject to a five-year automatic suspension for his actions.[100] The Elites missed his fastball during the stretch run.

The team nearly took over first place in the NNL in late August and would have done so had Joe Black not made a mistake in his pitch selection against the Philadelphia Stars in game two of a Bugle Field twin bill. After winning game one 7–1 behind the six-hit pitching of Andy Porter, the Elites took a 2–1 lead into the fourth inning of game two. With the bases loaded, former Elite now Stars manager Goose Curry put himself in as pinch hitter and cracked his favorite pitch—a shoulder high fastball from Black—into left center to drive in the second and third runs of the inning. The Elites managed only one more run.[101]

Another Labor Day doubleheader showdown between the Grays and the Elites at Griffith Stadium decided the 1945 second-half winner. The teams entered the contest tied at 12–6. Each needed to win both games to claim the pennant. Game one was not decided until the 12th inning, when Josh Gibson made it home on Jud Wilson's bloop double to left. Campanella, playing deep in left field to guard against an extra-base hit, was late retrieving Wilson's hit. Campanella's relay to Robinson and Robinson's relay home were too late to throw out Gibson, who scored the winning run. Until then, Jonas Gaines, in his first start for the Elites since returning from Army duty in Germany, had allowed only four hits, but the Grays had turned them into two runs. Welmaker, who also went the distance, allowed the Elites ten hits but only two runs. An Elites win in the nightcap would force a winner-take-all playoff, but that did not prove to be necessary. The Grays came out on top by taking the second game 5–3. Gibson's 420-foot homer was the difference.[102]

Losing both the first- and second-half pennants did not dampen the Elites' spirits in postseason play. They beat the Eagles before 8,000 at the Polo Grounds, in New York City, on September 30[103] and took six straight from the crosstown Baltimore Orioles in October. The O's had beefed up their squad for the occasion with two major leaguers—Washington Senators' pitcher Walt Masterson and the Athletics' second baseman Irving Hall—and Stars player Gene "Spider" Benson, Bill Ricks, and Ed Stone filled in for several missing Elites.[104]

Another temporary Oriole in these postseason games was Baltimore native Fred "Bunky" Trout, a nineteen-year-old pitcher who had spent the 1945 season with the Washington Senators' farm team in Greensboro, North Carolina, the Greensboro Patriots. Before signing with the Patriots, Trout had returned balls hit out of Bugle Field in exchange for free tickets. "I got to know Henry Kimbro that way," Trout said. "I used to work out with him, and he told me one day, 'If you ever get the chance to pitch to Campanella, change-up on him.' Well, I got my chance in that series [the six postseason games]. Roger Pippen, sports editor for the *Baltimore News American* asked me if I'd pitch for the all-stars. Of course I said yes, and over three games, thanks to Kimbro's advice, I struck Campanella out three times in a row in each game. He was so mad he called me 'a no shit white bastard.'"[105]

Others also knew about Campanella's weakness for the change-up. Monte Irvin, who played for the Eagles before signing with the New York Giants, said, "You had to know how to pitch to Campy. We used to pitch him inside and then throw a change-up off the plate by just that much [holding his thumb and forefinger a half-inch apart] to strike him out."[106]

During the last three years of the war, the Elites had failed to regain their 1942 form, but, thanks to the booming wartime economy, the team's finances had gotten a welcome boost. Cracks in the color bar, both in Baltimore's city life and in organized baseball, had appeared. More were on the way.

CHAPTER 4

Bending the Color Bar

Sparks Fly around Robinson and Rickey

By 1946 Negro leaguers were returning from the war to full-time baseball. The returnees included Elites and ex-Elites—Sammy T. Hughes, Joe Black, Bill Burns, Bill Harvey, Johnny Washington, and Frazier Robinson. A new war, the Cold War, got under way.[1] The employment picture dimmed for many, blacks and whites alike, in Baltimore's defense industries. Companies such as Glenn L. Martin Aircraft Company, Bethlehem-Fairfield Shipyards, and Eastern Aircraft had laid off a total of about 26,000 workers shortly after V-J Day in August of 1945. The job reductions continued into 1946. Because the layoffs were governed by seniority, blacks, being more recently hired, were more likely to be laid off.[2] When John C. Catlin, a black plumber, applied for a journeyman's license from the three-man licensing board appointed by Governor O'Conor, he encountered more racial discrimination. The board denied his application, as it had in 1941, for, among other reasons, the lack of a recommendation from a master plumber, all of whom were white. Black plumbers like Catlin had to work illegally on jobs requiring licenses.

In 1946 Branch Rickey signed more Negro leaguers to Dodger organization contracts. Roy Campanella was one of them. By late March, Snow, not having heard from Campanella, was worried about the catcher's position. Campanella was usually one of the first to report for spring training.[3] Rumors had the star backstop about to join the Dodgers organization as a member of the Danville, Illinois, farm club. Rickey, while not denying that the Dodgers were interested in Campanella, denied the specific rumor about Danville by saying, "None of the colored boys will be sent there."[4] Tom Wilson became convinced that the Dodgers would sign Campanella: Wilson had advanced Campanella $200 in the fall of 1945, and Campanella had recently mailed the money back to him in Nashville with no explanation.[5]

Finally, the secret that everyone knew was confirmed on Thursday, April 11, 1946, when Rickey signed Campanella to a contract with the Nashua, New Hampshire, club of the New England League. Rickey also signed Don Newcombe, from the Eagles, to a contract with the same club. Neither player returned reporters' phone calls to their homes.[6]

Though Campanella says little in his autobiography about his reaction to signing a major league contract, he had to be pleased. The Phillies had not offered him a contract, after suggesting they might. In 1942 he had received a letter from Pittsburgh Pirates president William Benswanger saying a tryout could be arranged, but the letter "had so many 'buts' in it," Campanella said, "I was discouraged even before I finished reading the letter." He nevertheless mailed a reply saying all the "buts" were fine with him. Receiving no reply, he decided, "I had been a fool to have built my hopes up so high against my better judgment."[7] Adding to Campanella's pleasure at the Dodgers contract was the fact that he had turned down an offer to sign with Rickey in October of 1945. After Rickey had signed Jackie Robinson but before he had announced the signing, he told Campanella that he had investigated dozens of Negro leaguers. Future Hall of Famer Oscar Charleston had investigated Campanella's background for Rickey and found it to be good. When asked by Rickey, "would you like to play for me?" Campanella said, "I'm doing all right where I am." Rickey said he understood and would get back in touch. He asked Campanella not to sign with another major league club without talking to him.

Campanella thought Rickey was asking him to play with the Brooklyn Brown Dodgers, a team created by Rickey to allay suspicion that he was scouting black players for the Dodgers, which he was. It was not until Campanella returned from his meeting with Rickey to the Woodside Hotel in Harlem, where Jackie Robinson and other players were awaiting a barnstorming tour of Venezuela, that he learned that Robinson had signed with the Dodgers.[8] Fearing that he had blown a chance to play in the majors, Campanella sent Rickey a telegram giving him their address in Venezuela. Rickey sent Campanella a telegram in early spring of 1946—when the season was wrapping up in Venezuela—asking him to report to the Dodger office by March 10. The telegram said it was "very important."[9]

Campanella's signing was not a financial windfall for him or the Elites. The Dodgers paid him a bonus of $2,400 but a monthly salary of only $185.[10] For the five-and-a-half-month season at Nashua his salary would amount to $1,017.50, substantially less than the $3,000 salary he earned with the Elites. Many told him he was making the biggest mistake of his life, but his wife, Ruthie, had urged him on, and he went to Nashua in high spirits.[11] Rickey made no payment to Wilson for Campanella's services, and Wilson let the issue pass. However, J. B. Martin, now owner of the Chicago American Giants and still Wilson's counterpart as president of the Negro American League, felt that owners were entitled to payment for their players. At the same time, Martin did not want such concerns to jeopardize a player's chance to make the majors. In an October 29, 1945, letter to Eagles' business manager Effa Manley, Martin said that he had the assurance of Tom Baird, KC Monarchs co-owner, "that whatever they [the Dodgers] offer for Robinson he will accept it. What we are trying to do is set up a principle for the others to follow. There will be no price named, for we are not going to jeopardize Robinson's chance. If they say $500.00 or $5,000.00, all well and good . . . BUT when they get other players, if they get them, we will place a reasonable price on them and demand it."[12] Rickey offered neither $500 nor $5,000 and signed Robinson without compensating Baird. Stars owner Ed Bolden took a more direct line with Rickey. Bolden asked for and got the modest sum of $1,000 for the signing of Stars pitcher Roy Partlow.

Effa Manley and Grays owner Cum Posey did not favor Bolden's strategy, but they did think that stronger measures than those proposed by Martin were needed. They wrote to Major League commissioner A. B.

"Happy" Chandler on November 1, 1945, expressing their belief that, "the clubs of Organized Negro Baseball who have gone to so much expense to develop players . . . should be approached and deals made." Posey and Manley invited Chandler to attend a meeting in New York to discuss the matter. Tom Wilson, in typical style, chose not to be involved in the planning. Posey and Manley said in their letter, "due to illness, our President Thomas T. Wilson will not be present, but he is in accord with our actions."[13]

The meeting took place in Cincinnati at the commissioner's office in the Carew Tower on January 24, 1946. Wilson was present after all, as was Martin. Also present, representing Major League Baseball, was an attorney, Herold "Muddy" Ruel, better known as a catcher for eighteen seasons with six American League teams. Chandler ignored the payment issues but suggested ways the Negro leagues could improve their business. He suggested that Negro league team owners build their own stadiums to reduce the fees paid to rent major league stadiums and that they pattern their player contracts after those in the majors, to prevent jumping and raiding. The owners passed on building stadiums, but within a month of the meeting they had printed contracts that were replicas of major league contracts, with the word "Negro" inserted where appropriate. Martin approved, saying, "The new contracts carry a reserve clause. It now appears that our contracts are about as ironclad as those of organized baseball."[14] A reserve clause amounted to a perpetual contract allowing the team to keep, trade, or sell a player regardless of his wishes. A series of court decisions rendered the clause unconstitutional in 1974.[15]

The new contracts had to be signed to be ironclad, and neither Campanella nor Newcombe had signed one with his Negro league team before signing with Rickey. While Manley was pleased that Newcombe had signed a major league contract, she felt that the Eagles should be compensated by the Dodgers, for the reason she had expressed to Chandler. Manley wrote several letters to Rickey protesting the lack of payment for Newcombe but received no answer.[16] She was mad. "Rickey took Robinson, Newcombe, and Campanella from our Negro baseball and didn't even say thank you," she said. "He took Newcombe from me, so I know what I'm talking about."[17]

For his part, Branch Rickey held the Negro leagues in contempt and therefore felt no call to bargain with the owners. Shortly after signing Robinson, Rickey said, "They are not leagues and have no right to expect organized baseball to respect them. They have the semblance of a racket."[18] He later elaborated on his opinion to Henry J. Walsh, an attorney for the Dodgers, to whom he wrote, "I felt both the American and Negro National League clubs were in the control of racketeers—men exploiting the colored players for their own purposes. They had no contracts, no league schedules and no constitution, and almost without exception, no written contracts with players." He said he had talked with people in both leagues to suggest that they remedy what Rickey felt the leagues were lacking but found, "My proposal was not at all acceptable."[19]

While integration of the majors continued and Baltimore's employment situation worsened, the Elites opened spring training in Nashville facing challenges at the plate and in the field. Wild Bill Wright's choice to play again in Mexico and Campanella's departure deprived the Elites of their two sluggers. The Elites' defense also needed improvement; they had led the NNL in errors in 1945.[20] Newcomers Luis Marquez (who ended up with the Grays), Jimmie Armistead, Stephen (Jim) Zapp, Luis Villodos, and Manuel Stewart joined the veterans for the Nashville workouts.[21]

While the Elites were playing exhibition games to get ready for the season, Jackie Robinson made his first appearance as a minor leaguer in Baltimore. Forty-five years earlier, a black player had attempted to play organized baseball in Baltimore, but under false pretenses. The disguise was removed when Charles Comiskey, owner of the Chicago White Sox, let it be known that Charlie Grant, another second baseman, whom John J. McGraw, manager of the Baltimore Orioles, wanted for the O's, was black, not the full-blooded Cherokee Indian that McGraw claimed him to be.[22]

Rickey did not misrepresent Robinson's ancestry, but he had passed over more skillful black players to choose Robinson. Acceptable personal traits and the personality to take the predictable barrage of insults without striking back were just as important considerations for Rickey as skill on the diamond. Rickey gave serious consideration to Josh Gibson, but Gibson's off-field behavior was unacceptable. Rickey did not consider Satchel Paige.[23] Paige's age and his love of the good life and the fair sex were, no doubt, well known to Rickey. As early as 1939, some Negro leaguers had expressed the same concerns. Elites manager Felton Snow said in a 1939 interview with reporter Sam Lacy, "We have so many guys who just wouldn't act right. There are so many men who get three or four dollars in their pockets and right away they want to tell 'the man' where he can go. It is quite a task finding the right combination. Many of the good players are bad actors and many ordinary players are fine characters."[24] Rickey decided Robinson had the right combination of talent and temperament.

Only 2,500 fans turned out on a chilly Saturday night to see Jackie Robinson's first game in Baltimore as a minor leaguer, but 25,306 paid customers, black and white, crammed into Municipal Stadium the next day, April 28, 1946, to see not only Robinson but also Montreal Royals black pitcher John Wright, formerly of the Grays, in a doubleheader.[25]

Fans in New Jersey had given Robinson a round of applause when the Royals faced the Jersey City Giants on April 18. The 25,000 fans who crowded into Roosevelt Stadium saw Robinson hit a three-run homer, rap out three singles, and make one error to lead the Royals to a 14–1 rout of the Giants. Jersey City fans fought to get into the Royals' clubhouse to congratulate Robinson. Before he reached the clubhouse well-wishers almost tore the jersey off his back and beseeched him for handshakes and autographs. Robinson reported that he was so excited that he had to tie his necktie three or four times to get it right.[26]

The response of the Baltimore crowd may have disconcerted Robinson for a different reason. International League president Frank Shaughnessy told Rickey several days before the games in Baltimore, "For God's sake, don't let him go." He described Baltimore's white fans as "up in arms." Rickey replied, "I don't think those awful things will happen. It's one more case of fearing trouble ahead."[27] But there was trouble ahead. The Orioles players said they would not play against Montreal, but Shaughnessy told them he would suspend them from baseball for life if they refused to take the field.[28] Robinson recounted that the white spectators "began screaming all the typical phrases such as 'nigger, son of a bitch.' Soon insults were coming from all over the stands."[29] Other insults, less vitriolic, were "Here comes the midnight express," "Who's that ink-spot," and "Who's that on second?"[30] Robinson said it was hardest on his wife, Rachel, who was "forced to sit in the midst of the hostile spectators." "She kept her temper," he said, "only because her dignity was more important to her than descending to the level of those ignorant bigots."[31] The harassment continued after the game, when large numbers of whites crowded around the door to the Royals' dressing room. As sports reporter and eyewitness Frank Lynch said, "They weren't after autographs." Police had to disperse the crowd.[32] By contrast, Robinson was the target of adulation from Baltimore's black fans, who ran onto the field, raised Robinson on their shoulders, and carried him in triumph around the field.[33]

Some years later, talking to *Afro-American* sports writer Sam Lacy, Robinson compared his receptions in Baltimore with the time when two players attempted to spike him during the Little World Series in Louisville, Kentucky, in the fall of 1946. "Baltimore was worse," Robinson told Lacy. "The nasty things Baltimore people threw at me hardened me to the point where this [the spiking] was rather easy to take . . . I knew I was coming into the South and I suppose I was preparing for just about anything, but that Baltimore, holy gee . . ."[34]

A week after Robinson's appearance at Municipal Stadium, the Elites opened their season at home on May 5th by splitting a doubleheader with the Grays.[35] McKeldin and Callaway teamed up once more on the ceremonial opening pitch.[36] The Elites moved on to Griffith Stadium on May 12th to face the Grays in front of 12,000 spectators. Bill Byrd gave Elite fans a ray of hope. He limited the Grays to six hits in six innings before rain ended the game in the seventh with the Elites ahead 4–1.[37] They struggled through the rest of May, however. By the end of the month, Wilson's men were in next-to-last place with a 5–7 record.[38]

In an effort to stem their losses, Wilson signed Willie Wells to play third and retrieved Sammy T. Hughes to play second. Wells, known as "The Devil" for his tenacious play, was at the end of his Hall of Fame career.[39] Hughes, who had been traded to the New York Black Yankees in September, had been holding out on New York since January in a salary dispute. Back with the Elites, Hughes played sporadically, then retired at the end of 1946, bringing to a close the career of one of the Negro leagues' greatest second basemen.[40] Vernon Green brought James "Junior" Gilliam up from the Nashville Black Vols to spell Hughes. George Scales told Gilliam at the time, "We got to have a second baseman to go with [shortstop] Butts. Sammy [Hughes] was alright but the army took it out of his legs. He can't get around. You try it, Junior."[41]

Gilliam's father had died when Junior was six months old. He and his mother, who took a job in a barbecue pit, lived with his maternal grandmother. By age 15 Gilliam was sweeping floors for Nashville's Woolworth store and playing baseball on a sandlot team, the Nashville Crawfords. The next year he played several months for the Nashville Black Vols of the Negro Southern League, an Elites farm team, earning $150 a month.[42] He got his nickname by being the youngest player on the club.

Scales, as he had done with Joe Black in 1943, worked with Gilliam to improve his skills. Scales taught the right-hander how to switch-hit and told him to spend the winter swinging a bat left-handed. "I told him to get one of those heavy DiMaggio bats to practice with."[43] Gilliam and Butts formed the best double-play combination in the Negro leagues during the late 1940s. "They were out of sight as a double play combination," said teammate Lenny Pearson. "Good hands, both of them, and both of them loved the game."[44]

The addition of Wells and Hughes infused new life into the team. Before 13,000 fans in Griffith Stadium on July 17, the Elites beat the Philadelphia Stars 3–2 and then turned around to beat the Kansas City Monarchs and their legendary pitcher, Satchel Paige. Scales smacked a triple, bringing in the run that broke the 3–3 tie.[45] The Elites moved into first place by beating the New York Black Yankees in a Sunday doubleheader, 7–3 and 9–1.[46] They went on to win four straight games, bringing their league-game winning streak to seven. Joe Black, just released from his stateside military duty, beat the New York Cubans 5–2 at Bugle Field.

The Elites were now tied with the Newark Eagles, winner of the first-half pennant, for the second-half lead.[47]

Then, an all-too-familiar scenario reasserted itself. In an August 11th Sunday afternoon game at the Polo Grounds, the New York Cubans beat the Elites before 11,000 fans. Elite pitchers Byrd, Black, and Enrique Figueroa gave up ten hits. The loss dropped the Elites into third place.[48] They played under .500 ball the rest of the way home and ended the second half in third place.

As the Elites struggled to achieve a third-place finish, a power shift occurred atop the Negro National League standings. The Newark Eagles, often a middle-of-the-pack team, put together a 15–2 run at the end of the season to win the second-half pennant and the season pennant by virtue of having clinched the first-half flag. The Cubans had their best season in years with a second-place finish. The Homestead Grays, uncharacteristically, struggled to avoid the cellar. They finished the second half in fourth place at 9–13, their worst second-half finish since 1935.[49]

Other than Gilliam's and Butts's performances, neither the Elites as a team nor any individual players had much to cheer about. Wilson relieved Felton Snow of his responsibilities as the Elites' manager and assigned him to pilot the Nashville Vols in 1947.[50]

Wilson Ousted

Wilson's tenure as Negro National League president ended in January 1947. He had considered resigning at the end of the 1945 season due to poor health.[51] He had offered to resign in 1946, but the other owners, except for the Manleys, insisted that he stay on.[52] Effa Manley, still adamant in her opposition to Wilson as president, faulted the owners for their lack of truthfulness. In a letter to Cum Posey dated January 12, 1946, she wrote, "Several of the members got hold of Tom and asked him not to resign . . . I can't understand how people can be so deceitful. Behind his back they all say they want someone else for Chairman, but no one will say it to his face."[53]

On January 5th at the owners' winter meeting in the Theresa Hotel in New York, four of the six owners said it to his face. The Manleys, Grays owners Rufus Jackson and Mrs. Ethel Posey (Cum Posey had died the previous year), the New York Cubans' Alex Pompez, and the Black Yankees' James and Maude Semler voted against Wilson and for Effa's hand-picked candidate, Rev. John H. Johnson, pastor of St. Martin's Episcopal Church at 122nd Street and Lenox Avenue in New York City. Only the Stars' Ed Bolden voted with Wilson.[54] Effa finally got her way.

A contributing factor in the owners' decision to oust Wilson was Rickey's and Chandler's suggestion that the Negro leagues would appear more respectable to major leagues if the league president was not also a team owner.[55] There had been clear conflicts of interest. Wilson, while league president, had occasion to rule on matters affecting the Elites. Game one of a doubleheader between the Elites and the Grays in September 1940 that would decide the second-half pennant was one example. The Grays delayed the start of the game for twenty minutes protesting Kimbro's presence in the Elites' line-up. Kimbro had been ejected from a game the previous week against the Stars for starting a fight. Grays officials argued that Kimbro should have also received a suspension, which would have made him ineligible for this game. Umpire E. C. Turner approached Wilson for a ruling. Kimbro went one for six that afternoon.[56]

One of the people pleased that Wilson lost the league presidency must have been his Nashville physician, Dr. R. B. Jackson. He had counseled Wilson to resign for health reasons.[57] Little could be found on the state of Wilson's health during his career save for a statement that he underwent surgery of an unspecified nature in December 1938.[58]

The Rev. John Johnson, 40, had no previous experience with professional baseball other than his two-year chairmanship of New York mayor Fiorello La Guardia's Mayor's Committee on Baseball, but he had long actively worked to benefit black New Yorkers. The purpose of the mayor's committee was to study discrimination in organized baseball.[59] Johnson, by his own admission, knew little about baseball but did offer the quality of independence. He said at the end of the meeting where the owners elected him that he "did not feel the need for counsel from the club owners."[60]

The same month that Wilson was voted out as president, a significant step on the path to racial integration happened in Baltimore. Police Commissioner Hamilton R. Atkinson promoted plainclothes detective J. Hiram Butler Jr. to the rank of sergeant—along with forty-eight white officers—making him the force's first black sergeant. Butler had been one of the first three blacks appointed to the force, in 1938. By the time of his promotion, nine years later, there were twelve black officers.[61]

With the election over, Wilson and Green worked on the roster for 1947. Wilson hired Wes Barrow, who had managed the Nashville Vols the previous year, to manage the Elites. Barrow was not well known in eastern baseball circles, having spent his twenty-one years with teams in the Deep South as a player and manager.[62] As was his custom, Wilson did not explain his choice of Barrow to the press. Following Barrow's hiring, Green announced that six new players had been invited to spring training in Nashville. Among them were Robert "Butch" Davis, whose bat would be a welcome addition to the line-up, and Joe Wiley. Wiley was scheduled to share second base duties with Junior Gilliam. Wiley saw little action. In another move to shore up the team, Wilson traded aging Willie Wells to the Indianapolis Clowns for Lester Lockett, who would play three years for the Elites, mostly in the outfield, and make the All-Star team in 1948.[63]

A confident Elite Giants team opened the 1947 season against the Stars in Philadelphia on a chilly Saturday, May 3, before only 2,000 fans, who no doubt got colder watching the Elites rout the Stars 20–4. Kimbro led the way with two homers, two doubles, and a running catch that robbed Stars first baseman Wesley Dennis of a home run. Byrd went the distance for the Elites. Word of their win brought a standing-room-only opening day crowd of 6,985 paid fans to Bugle Field to watch the Elites and Stars split a doubleheader. Newcomer Bob Romby and veteran Joe Black combined to yield four runs to the Stars in the opener, while their teammates produced only one. Kimbro got his third homer of the series in game two, which the Elites won 7–2.[64]

Twelve days later, Tom Wilson died of a heart attack, at age 61, on his farm twelve miles outside of Nashville, at 11:00 p.m., just four months after being voted out of the league presidency. The funeral was held at the St. Paul A.M.E. Church at the corner of Fourth Avenue and Franklin Street in Nashville on May 19. His mother, Dr. Carry Wilson, his wife, Thelma, his son, Thomas T. Wilson Jr., and his daughter, Christine Wilson Childs, survived him.[65]

Wilson's death brought a new manager to the team. According to catcher Frazier Robinson, Wesley Barrow "was Tom Wilson's man, and Fat Daddy [Green] didn't think too much of Barrow."[66] So Green called Felton Snow back from Nashville to pilot the Elites through the rest of the '47 season.[67]

Thanks to excellent pitching, the Elites were in second place by the end of May, a game and a half behind the Newark Eagles. The first-half pennant race between the Elites and Eagles tightened as June wore on. Romby lost a three-hitter to the Grays, 1–0. Six walks overshadowed his otherwise stellar performance. On June 24th the Elites and Eagles faced off at Brooklyn's Ebbets Field, the Elites winning handsomely, 16–7. Pee Wee Butts collected four hits and scored three runs. The Elites' win put them in first place, but not for long. When the first half of the season came to a close, the Eagles were on top at 25–13. The Elites were, once again, close behind in second place, this time with a 23–16 record. They had improved their fielding markedly from the year before, boasting the second best fielding percentage behind only the Stars. They were also the best hitting team in the NNL, rapping the ball at a .299 team clip.

Five Elites—pitchers Bob Romby and Joe Black, shortstop Pee Wee Butts, first baseman Johnny Washington, and center fielder Henry Kimbro—were selected for the July 29 All-Star Game at the Polo Grounds.

Three weeks before the All-Star Game, Cleveland Indians owner Bill Veeck had signed Larry Doby of the Eagles, on July 5, 1947, making Doby the first player of color in the American League.[68] The black press increased its coverage of the black players now in organized baseball, and gave proportionately less coverage to the Negro leagues. The *Baltimore Afro-American*, for instance, in addition to regular articles on Doby, Rob-

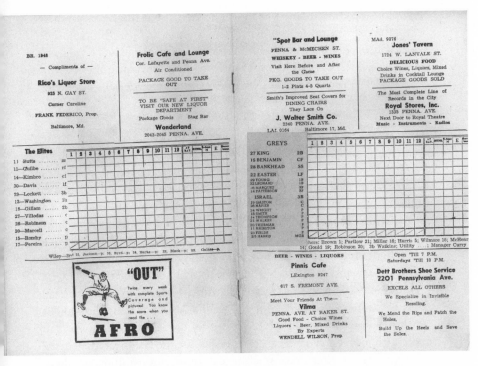

The score sheet from a 1947 Elites program for a game against the Grays. The Giants pasted the opposing team's line-up into the program to reduce printing costs.

inson, and Campanella, ran a column titled "Following the Stars," which gave a day-by-day accounting of what they did.

The coverage that was given to NNL games for the second half of the '47 season documented an Elites decline. By the first of August, the New York Cubans led the league; they had come up winners against the Elites in 8 of the 12 games between the two teams. The Cubans made it 9 of 13 with a 10–5 win in the Polo Grounds on August 3. The Cubans' lead over the Elites grew to 11 out of 15 with a doubleheader won 5–4 and 5–3 at Bugle Field on Sunday, August 10. As fate would have it, the Grays and Elites met again in the last game of the season but there were no championships on the line this time. The Grays sent the Elites on their postseason barnstorming tour with a 4–0 shutout at Griffith Stadium.[69]

The Elites closed out 1947 with Vernon Green as the team's owner and sole stockholder. Wilson had sold Green a half-interest in the team in March 1947. Wilson's son, Thomas T. Wilson Jr., inherited the other half from his father and sold it to Green.[70]

The year came to a close with employment figures well below those of the war years for both whites and blacks in Baltimore, but that did not stop them from playing the numbers to the tune of about $50,000 a day. Whites controlled the games in South Baltimore and East Baltimore, while the bosses were black in Old West, where they numbered about a dozen. These men, called "bankers," took in $3,000 to $5,000 in receipts a day. To play the numbers a person placed a bet in the form of three single-digit numbers, such as 692, with a writer, who met a pick-up man between noon and one o'clock. The pick-up man took the money and the numbers to the banker's headquarters, which could be an office, kitchen table, or dining room, depending on the banker's finances. Throughout the process, lookout men kept an eye out for the police, both uniformed and undercover. Each day bankers agreed to use the results of three horse races at an East Coast race track to determine the winning numbers. They totaled the parimutuel payout on the horses that won, placed, and showed in each of the three races. Say those totals came to $26.30 for the first race, $29.70 for the second race, and $22.00 for the third race. The bankers selected the number in the units place in each total—in this case 6, 9, and 2—to determine the winning combination. The payoff to a winning player depended on the amount bet. A big enough bet on a winning number could bring a player enough to buy a house. Successful bankers often invested their money in legitimate businesses, including Negro league baseball teams. Many in the numbers business were, according to one account, "ardent sports fans, who dressed flashily, carried wads of money, owned sporty automobiles, and threw money away on fast women."[71]

Baltimore entrepreneur Clarence Brown said, "The only way Negroes could buy a home was to hit their numbers. Everybody wrote numbers, but you could get locked up. You only wrote numbers for people you thought you knew. No whites—they were [undercover] police. Then they put a Negro on the police force and they'd bust you. It was a $500 fine the first time and $1,000 for twice."[72]

Wilson's death left the Elites without the guidance of the man who had founded the original team, in Nashville in 1921; but their play on the field improved over that of recent years, and many thought the team was poised for a stellar year in 1948.

A Near Miss

By 1948 Theodore McKeldin had lost his mayoral reelection bid to Democrat Thomas D'Alessandro Jr., who went on record, in the tradition of McKeldin, at the annual January meeting of the Advertising Club of Baltimore, as calling for an end to racial and religious intolerance.[73] That much needed to be done in that regard could be seen in the fact that the same eleven women's apparel stores that had discriminated against black customers in 1945 still maintained that policy. A young African American boy was forcibly removed from a line of children waiting to see Santa Claus at Stewart's department store during the 1947 Christmas season. In a change from 1945, though, some more open-minded clerks in these eleven stores ignored their store's policy and served black women.[74]

Other signs of progress in racial equality included the U.S. Supreme Court's decision on May 3, 1948, in *Shelley v. Kraemer* that restrictive housing covenants based on race or religion were unconstitutional. The Court's decision opened up a range of housing options far beyond anything that had been available to Baltimore's black citizens to date. Incidents of violence directed by whites toward blacks who bought into white neighborhoods still occurred, nevertheless. One involved two white men who set off a large rocket that destroyed parts of a house at 205 North Pine Street. A white seaman set fire to a three-story house at nearby 713 West Fayette Street in West Baltimore, then tried to prevent the occupants, three black families, from leaving the house. The seaman died of gunshot wounds.[75] Progress was apparent in the Fulton Avenue area of Old West, where whites and blacks were living peacefully together a month after the Court's decision. Four years before, white Fulton Avenue residents had demanded that Mayor McKeldin end the "block busting" caused by black war workers' and veterans' buying homes on Fulton.[76]

The Elites experienced changes as well in 1948. Left-handed pitcher Bill Harvey retired from the Elites and landed a job in Baltimore with Bethlehem Steel.[77] Former Elites southpaw Tom Glover died June 7 at the Henryton (Maryland) Sanatorium, located on Henryton Road near Patapsco State Park west of Baltimore City. The cause of death was not reported but the sanatorium was known for its treatment of tuberculosis. Abandoned in 1985, the deserted structure is a favorite haunt of modern-day ghost seekers.[78] The team would be in the thick of the pennant race down to the last game of each half of the season. The Elites were poised to do well, but attendance throughout the Negro leagues was declining as the financial pressures brought on by integration of organized baseball continued to depress ticket sales.

Green signed "Candy" Jim Taylor to manage the Elites. Taylor had over twenty years experience as a manager with many teams, including the Elites when they were in Nashville (1933–34), Columbus (1935), and Washington (1936) and the St. Louis Stars, the Washington-Homestead Grays, and the Chicago American Giants.[79] Felton Snow, who knew something about managing, considered Taylor to be the greatest strategist in baseball.[80]

Taylor came from a South Carolina family of five brothers, four of whom were among the biggest stars in Negro league baseball—Jim, Ben, C.I., and Johnny. Ben was the only other Taylor brother with a Baltimore connection. In addition to playing for the Baltimore Black Sox and later owning the Baltimore Stars, Ben, at the time of Candy Jim's hiring by Green, ran a pool hall in Baltimore and handled scorecard sales at the Elites' home games.[81] Ben owned and operated a pool hall, Ben's Sports Center, at 1917 Pennsylvania Avenue in Old West, from 10 a.m. until midnight.[82] He died in Baltimore in January of 1953.

Candy Jim was ill in a Chicago hospital when spring training opened

Elites pitcher Bill Harvey, 1947

in Nashville in late March, but was expected to report in several days. Green appointed veteran outfielder Kimbro to be the team's temporary manager. All the regulars from the previous season were in camp except first baseman Johnny Washington, who was holding out for more money.[83] A week into spring training, Jim Taylor died.[84] No details have been found on the nature of his illness other than it was not considered serious at its onset. The Elite players were reported to be mourning the loss of "one of the most popular and best loved veterans in baseball."[85] Green then hired Jesse "Hoss" Walker to manage the team. Walker had played shortstop for the Elites from 1931 to 1938 and continued his playing career until 1943 with several teams. He had managed the Indianapolis Clowns off and on from 1943 to 1946.

On the player front, Green promoted 21-year-old first baseman Clinton "Butch" McCord, who was attending Tennessee State College, from the Vols to the Elites. McCord was reported to be "the most promising youngster seen around an Elite training camp since 'Pee Wee' Butts came up in 1939." Whether Johnny Washington had heard about McCord's promotion is not known, but Washington ended his holdout a few days after McCord signed.[86]

The Elites now had a solid team capable of contending for the NLL flag. The infield, with Washington at first, Gilliam at second, Butts at short, and rookie Mike Finney from the Akron, Ohio, sandlots at third was one of the league's best. The outfield consisted of Kimbro, the Cuban winter league batting champ, in center, Lester Lockett in left, and Frankie Russell and Butch McCord alternating in right. Bill Byrd, Joe Black, and Bob Romby composed an impressive starting pitching rotation. Frazier Robinson completed the battery.[87]

The Elites started slowly, dropping their May 2 opener to the Eagles 2–1. Congressman Edward A. Garmatz, a white Democrat from Maryland's 3rd District took the mound before the game started and slipped three pitches past traditional opening ceremonies catcher, Republican businessman Marse Callaway.[88] Two days later they fell again to the Eagles by the same 2–1 score.[89] They came back to beat the Cubans in both ends of a Yankee Stadium doubleheader, 3–2 and 9–6, on May 18. Joe Black relieved Jonas Gaines in game one and pitched game two until

Elites right fielder Clinton "Butch" McCord circa 1948 on Pennsylvania Avenue

Romby relieved him. About 5,000 fans saw the games, noticeably fewer than the 10,000–15,000 fans who had turned out for Sunday double-headers at Yankee Stadium only a year or two earlier.

Butts provided some extra excitement in game one by taking exception to home plate umpire Julio Hernandez's change of mind on a call. Hernandez called "trapped" and then "caught" a line drive Butts hit to left field. Butts struck Hernandez, knocked him down, and jumped on him. This was the normally quiet Butts's first run-in with an umpire. League president Johnson suspended Butts for ten games and fined him $100.[90]

The Elites did well in June and were in second place behind the Grays as of June 27th. The Elites beat the Black Yankees in both games of a doubleheader for their fourth straight win. A week later they continued their winning ways, taking a four-game series from the Stars. Bill Byrd, newly arrived Ernest Burke, Joe Black, and Bob Romby gained the wins for the Elites. Butts, Lockett, Kimbro, and Washington led the way at the plate. When the fourth game ended, the Elites had passed the Grays to take a one-half game lead in the standings.[91]

Having overcome their so-so start to the season, the Elites met the Grays in the last game of the first half tied for the lead. This time the Elites emerged victorious, nailing down the first-half flag.[92]

The Elites would have their first NNL championship since 1939 if they could win the second-half race. They would have been leading the league come August had they not lost three out of four games during the last week of July.

Once again, the race for the second-half flag came down to the Grays and the Elites. The Grays did the Elites a favor by knocking off the Stars in five straight games in the last week of the season. The Elites helped themselves by also defeating the Stars in two games, behind the pitching of Byrd and Black and the bats of Kimbro and Russell. Byrd furthered his own cause in the second game by knocking in the winning run.[93]

One press account of the second-half results reported that the Grays had moved to within one half game of the Elites by winning game one of a Labor Day doubleheader between the two teams in Baltimore.[94] One is left to presume that the Grays won game two as well, for they were declared the second-half winners.

Catcher Frazier Robinson, however, recalled the Elites winning both halves of the season, not just the first half. Robinson concluded that the Grays' Sonnyman Jackson, who had run the team since Posey's death the year before, had convinced NNL President Johnson to order a playoff, which Robinson considered to be unfair.[95] Whether Jackson pressured Johnson to order a playoff is not known, but the Grays and Elites did meet each other in a playoff series. The Grays, as described in the Prologue, won the series as a result of Umpire Lewis's not knowing the rules.

The Grays' championship was that team's final moment of glory. Falling attendance forced the Grays and New York Black Yankees to fold and the Eagles to change owners and cities after the 1948 season. The Grays did play as an independent, non-league team the next year before folding altogether. Effa and Abe Manley ended one of the most colorful chapters in the history of the Negro leagues when they sold the Newark Eagles to Dr. W. H. Young of Memphis, Tennessee, and Hugh Cherry of Blytheville, Arkansas. The new owners moved the team to Houston, Texas.[96] The remaining three NNL teams, the Elites, Stars, and New York Cubans, along with the new Houston team, joined the six-team Negro American League.[97] Officials dissolved the Negro National League, which Rube Foster had founded in 1920.[98] NNL president Johnson returned to full-time ministering. J. B. Martin retained the NAL presidency.

Financial pressure was nothing new to Negro league baseball, but money was becoming increasingly scarce for two reasons. The end of the war had brought with it a decline in jobs, leaving large numbers of blacks unemployed. Where crowds of 12,000–18,000 were once common for Negro league Sunday doubleheaders at Yankee Stadium, the Polo Grounds, and Griffith Stadium, 5,000 became the expected crowd by 1948. Attendance figures for the Newark Eagles were another case in point. Over the course of the 1946 season, 120,293 filled the seats in Ruppert Stadium. Just one year later, the figure dropped to 57,119. As of the first week of September in 1948, only 32,000 had bought tickets.[99] Secondly, many black fans with money for baseball tickets were spending their baseball dollars on major league games, to watch the likes of Robinson, Campanella, and Doby. On April 15, 1947, when Robinson trotted from the dugout to his position at first base, blacks made up 60 percent of the 25,623 spectators at Ebbets Field. Before that day they had usually accounted for 10 percent of the attendance at Ebbets Field.[100]

In response to the financial downturn, NNL owners decided that total teams' salaries were not to exceed $8,000 a month. Most owners cut players' salaries, by about $100 a month. The cuts had two effects on players. Many, feeling underpaid, performed indifferently; and some, like Johnny Davis (Eagles), "Groundhog" Thompson (Grays), and Sylvio Garcia (Cubans), jumped to Mexico or South America. The Elites did not experience such problems. No one jumped, and play continued at a high level because Vernon Green took a different financial stance. He cut the number of players, from twenty-five to twenty, so that the remaining twenty continued to receive their full salary.[101]

Amidst the changes, the Negro league ballpark still continued to run a close second to the church as a place where blacks were free to enjoy themselves without the restraints imposed by segregation, discrimination, and poverty. Dan Burley, a black sportswriter for the *New York Amsterdam News*, put it this way: "When you think of the mothers and fathers and youngsters who spend most of their lives either at work or in dingy, dark . . . apartments, squeezed in like sardines, having to choose between church and saloon as the major places of inspiration, diversion, or entertainment, you see what Negro baseball has meant over the years."[102]

The new ten-team Negro American League had two divisions, East and West. The Elites, New York Cubans, Philadelphia Stars, Indianapolis Clowns, and Louisville Buckeyes (formerly the Cleveland Buckeyes) composed the Eastern Division. The Chicago American Giants, Memphis Red Sox, Kansas City Monarchs, Birmingham Black Barons, and Houston Eagles called the Western Division home.[103]

The demise of the Grays and the Yankees left their players unattached. To avoid a bidding war, NAL president Martin established a lottery system for drafting players from both teams by drawing numbers out of a hat. Baltimore got third choice and drafted outfielder Luis Marquez and pitcher Roy Welmaker from the Grays and pitcher John Davidson of the Yanks.[104]

Welmaker, who was playing in Venezuela when drafted by the Elites, opted for a walk-on tryout with the Cleveland Indians in the spring of 1949. He made a favorable impression on manager Lou Boudreau, who signed him to a contract. Welmaker played for several years in the minors before retiring in 1953.[105] Marquez, a native of Aquadilla, Puerto Rico, became the first Elite Giant since Campanella to be signed by organized baseball when Green sold him to the New York Yankees, who assigned his contract to the Newark Bears. Marquez was the first "tan" player signed by the New York Yankee organization.[106] But Marquez never played for the Bears or the Yankees. Commissioner Chandler ruled that a deal had been struck between Cleveland Indians owner Bill Veeck and Grays business manager S. H. Posey (Cum Posey's brother) before Elites president Vernon Green selected Marquez and agreed to sell him to the Yankees, so Marquez belonged to the Indians.[107] He played in the minor leagues for several years before seeing limited major league action with the Boston Braves in 1951 and Chicago Cubs and Pittsburgh Pirates in 1954.[108] Davidson pitched for the Elites in 1950.[109]

While narrowly losing the Negro National League pennant, the 1948 Elites had their best year since 1942. Things were not looking good for Negro league baseball in general. Fault lines in the league's financial structure were becoming more prominent.

Finally!

One of the owners' first moves before the 1949 season got under way was to once again rescind a ban they had placed on players who jumped to teams south of the border. This amnesty allowed such Negro league stars as Leon Day, Bill Wright, Ray Dandridge, Ted Radcliffe, and Art Pennington to return to the States.[110] Day, a resident of West Baltimore, was one who did. Vernon Green wasted no time acquiring him from the Houston Eagles through a trade for Jonas Gaines.[111] Renowned as a pitcher during his career with the Newark Eagles but advancing in years, Day was still a threat at the plate. Green used him as a utility player.[112]

In a unique and luxurious move, given the deteriorating finances, Green hired Grays manager, Vic Harris, the Negro league's premier strategist, as a coach for the Elites. Harris was not expected to play but to devote his full attention to improving players' skills.[113] Press reports speculated that Hilton Smith of the Kansas City Monarchs might be added to the Elites' roster, but, unfortunately for the Elites, the reports were false.[114] Green traded first baseman Johnny Washington for Eagles first baseman Lenny Pearson and bought catcher Johnny Hayes from the

Baltimore pitcher
Al "Apples" Wilmore

Kansas City Monarchs.[115] Opting for continuity in the manager's job, he re-signed Hoss Walker.[116] Right-handed pitcher Ernest Burke was the only starting member of the 1948 squad to be released.[117]

The Elites opened their season on Sunday, May 8th with double-header wins 6–3 and 5–0 against the Indianapolis Clowns at Bugle Field. Second-year pitcher Alfred "Apples" Wilmore and Romby limited the Clowns to five hits in each game. The Elites followed up with a 5–3 win over the Monarchs the following Tuesday. The Monarchs came back with a 4–2 win over the Elites in Chester, Pennsylvania, on Wednesday and a 5–4 victory in Griffith Stadium the following evening. Leroy

Leon Day

"Stubs" Ferrell led the Elites to a series-tying 3–2 win over the Monarchs on Friday at Bugle Field.[118]

A week later, the Elites scored a Bugle Field trifecta at the expense of the Stars. Joe Black out-pitched Barney Brown for a 5–2 win on Saturday night May 14. Leon Day played center field and contributed a triple. The Elites took both Sunday games, with Byrd and Romby getting the wins. Butch Davis led the Elites batsmen with a 4 for 7 day at the plate.

The Elites were hot, but Green had no official indication of where they stood in the standings. The problem of spotty recordkeeping had not been solved, as not all NAL teams reported the game scores to a central location. Green was upset by this situation, since by his reckoning the Elites should be in first place. He threatened to pull the Elites from the league, saying, "Something must be done about it if we are to continue our affiliation with this league."[119] Something evidently was done, for the Elites continued in the league.

In the midst of the team's success on the field, Vernon Green, at age 49, succumbed to heart problems on May 29 at Provident Hospital in Baltimore. Ownership of the Elites passed to his wife, Henryene.[120] She gave Richard Powell, the Elites' business manager following Wilson's death, power of attorney and the titles of general manager and vice-president.[121]

The Elites were in second place in the Eastern Division behind the New York Cubans as the middle of June approached. The Elites swept another twin bill on June 12, edging the Chicago American Giants 5–4 in both games. Leon Day's two-run homer in the seventh inning of game one nullified Chicago's 4–3 lead.[122] The Elites gave another boost to their first-half flag hopes by duplicating their twin bill feat a week later, also at Bugle Field, against the division-leading Cubans. Byrd and Black pitched victories of 3–1 and 9–0. Lockett's two home runs over the left field fence in game one were the Elites' offensive highlights.[123]

The Elites ganged up on the Cubans over the July 4th weekend at Bugle Field to produce thirty-nine hits while sweeping the three-game series and winning the first-half Eastern Division flag. Byrd, now 42, was magnificent in relief of Wilmore in Friday night's game and of Romby in Sunday's opener.[124]

Once again the question was, What about the second half? Twenty-year-old rookie pitcher Sylvester Rogers from El Dorado, Arkansas, got the Elites off to a fast start. He threw eight innings of four-hit ball against the New York Cubans en route to an Elites 3–2 win in Trenton, New Jersey, on July 12th. Joe Black came on in the ninth to ensure the win. After the game, the Elites headed southward for a two-week tour to face the Memphis Red Sox, Birmingham Black Barons, and Kansas City Monarchs.[125]

Shortly after the tour started, four Elites gained berths on the Eastern Division squad for the East-West All-Star Game in Chicago's Comiskey

Park on August 14. At that game, major league commissioner Happy Chandler threw out the first ball, becoming the first major league official to throw the ceremonial pitch at any Negro league game. Butch Davis started in left field, while three of the four infield positions were manned by Elites: Butts at short, Gilliam at second, and Pearson at first. The East shut out the West 4–0. Butts and Davis scored a run apiece and Gilliam drove in a run with a sacrifice fly. It was the East squad's first win in seven years.[126]

With the four all-stars leading the way, the Elites continued to play well. Coverage by the *Afro-American* was limited to a few games, but the big news came in the September 15th edition, which announced that the Elites had won the second-half flag, making them "the official and undisputed champions of the Eastern Division."[127] The Elites would play the Western Division champs, the Chicago American Giants, for the championship of the Negro American League. With five Elites batting over .300 (Gilliam, Kimbro, Davis, Pearson, and Finney), the Elites were the favorites in the best-four-out-of-seven series.[128]

They started fast by beating the Chicago Giants in games one and two at Bugle Field by scores of 9–1 on Friday night, September 16, and 5–4 two days later in a Sunday afternoon game. Byrd held the Chicago nine to seven scattered hits on Friday, while Pearson led the Elites' offense with two singles and a double. Thanks to his teammates, Joe Black survived despite giving up sixteen hits to the opposition on Sunday.[129]

Sunday's game was the last ever played at Bugle Field. The Gallagher Realty Company had sold Bugle Field to the Lord Baltimore Press in July of 1947,[130] but the printing and bookbinding firm had waited more than two years, until September 19, 1949, to dismantle the structures on the field.[131] A distribution center for Mars Super Markets occupies the site of Bugle Field as of this writing.

The teams played game three in Norfolk, Virginia, on Monday. The Elites won 8–4.[132] The Chicago nine hosted the fourth game in the Windy City on Wednesday at Comiskey Park. The game was scoreless until the top of the sixth, when Butts singled, moved to second on an error that landed Kimbro on first, and scored on a double to right by Pearson that sent Kimbro to third. Chicago pitcher Gentry Jessup's throw to home after fielding an infield tap by Davis caught Kimbro at the plate. Davis stole second. Then Leon Day doubled to right, scoring Pearson and Davis for a 3–0 Elite lead. The Elites scored once more in the eight. Chicago scored two runs in the ninth, but then the rally fizzled. The Elites won the game 4–2, behind the six-hit pitching of Apples Wilmore, and were the champions of the Negro American League.[133]

Elites manager Hoss Walker was not around for the on-field celebration. He had taken issue with umpire Virgil Blueitt's call that the Elites' Henry Kimbro was out at home and he had shoved Blueitt and refused to leave the field when Blueitt gave him the heave-ho. Two of Chicago's finest escorted Walker to the Elites' locker room. Walker's antics cost him a $50 fine and a ten-day suspension, to be served the following year.[134]

After so many years of making spirited runs at the championship only to be bested in the stretch run, the Elites finally had a world championship to savor. But only the players celebrated. There were no parades in the Monumental City, celebrity-laced trophy presentations, or other outpourings of civic celebration. McCord remembers the players celebrating after the last game. "Some had some beer. We didn't throw the beer on each other. We drank the beer. I drank OJ."[135]

Not much had changed on the racial front in Baltimore or elsewhere in Maryland. Legislatures in other states, however, were moving forward. New Mexico, Rhode Island, and Washington had adopted bills banning discrimination in employment. Connecticut, Illinois, Wisconsin, and New York had outlawed segregation in National Guard units. Encouraged by the efforts in those states, Albert L. Sklar, a black Fourth District member of Maryland's House of Delegates, introduced a resolution that the body study discrimination in state agencies. The resolution died a quiet death in the House Committee on Licensing Boards and Commissions.[136] On a positive note, the State Board of Plumbing finally awarded a journeyman plumber's license to John Catlin who had been refused a license in 1941 and in 1946 by the same board. Catlin, the city's first black journeyman plumber, attributed his success on this third try to the fact that membership on the board had recently changed.[137]

World Champion 1949 Baltimore Elite Giants. Standing, left to right: *Joe Black, Leroy Ferrell, John Davidson, Lenny Pearson, Bill Byrd, Al Wilmore, Bob Romby, Johnny Hayes, Junior Gilliam, Hoss Walker.* Seated, left to right: *Butch Davis, Lester Lockett, Sylvester Rogers, Henry Kimbro, Vic Harris, Henry Bayliss, Frazier Robinson, Frank Russell, Pee Wee Butts, Leon Day.*

The loss of Bugle Field and the ongoing financial shortfalls tempered the Elites' elation over winning a long-sought world championship. More challenges lay ahead.

Moving and Moving On

Following the demolition of Bugle Field, Matt Reinhold of Gallagher Realty Company informed Richard Powell that the company owned a plot of land in the Westport section of Baltimore, a few blocks south of where Camden Yards, home of today's Baltimore Orioles, now sits, where a ballpark could be built. Reinhold said he thought the Westport location was "good enough for Negroes."[138] In addition to uttering such disparaging remarks, Reinhold was at times unresponsive to the team's requests of him. Green asked Powell in a 1947 letter, "What is Matt doing about the park? I wanted bleachers in the outfield. Since then, I received a letter from Ben [Taylor] saying he is moving the fence in instead of him building bleachers back to the fence as he promised."[139] The fences may have been moved in, but the bleachers were never built. Reinhold was more responsive to Powell's need for a ballpark and arranged for an "earthen and concrete stadium to be built on a hillside next to Old Annapolis Road."[140]

The new structure was small, uninviting, completed late, and a stadium in name only. On the team's stationery, the name appeared as Westport Baseball Park, a more descriptive title.[141] The grandstand had no roof; the field was rough. Powell was so upset with Westport that he said, "I can't find words to say how bad it was. It only looked like a baseball diamond. It had no infield grass, and a constant wind stirred up the grit."[142]

Motorists trying to reach the park were forced to drive through an ill-marked detour.[143] Annapolis Road was unlit, making it a dangerous walk to the park from the transit company's closest stop, the end of Trolley Line 17, about a half-mile from the park.[144] The other public transportation line, the Baltimore and Annapolis Railway, charged patrons the full round-trip Baltimore-to-Annapolis bus fare of fifty cents for stopping at the park on the way to Annapolis.[145]

Concerned about Westport's 2,000-seat capacity, Powell approached the Baltimore City Park Board, which controlled Memorial Stadium, to ask about renting it for seventeen dates. Perhaps remembering the 1942 fight in the stands at Oriole Park, the board's chairman, Dr. Bernard Harris, was concerned there would be trouble. Powell assured Harris there would be no trouble and agreed to Harris's demand that monitors be present to, in Powell's words, "make sure we didn't tear the place up." The board did agree to lease the stadium to the Elites, for seven dates ("three Sundays, four Fridays, and one alternate rain date with the understanding that doubleheaders could be played on Friday or Sunday"), ten fewer than Powell had asked for.[146] The rent was steep, "fifteen per-cent of the gross (after Federal and State Admission taxes) or $500.00 minimum, whichever is greater."[147] In turning down Powell's request for seventeen dates, the Park Board issued a statement saying, "We haven't reached the point where the Elites represent the city of Baltimore as by custom the Orioles do."[148]

Following his negotiation with Harris, Powell convened the team in Charlotte, North Carolina, for spring training. Pearson took over as manager from Walker, who became owner and manager of the Nashville Vols.[149] Good news for Powell arrived in the form of an offer by the Chi-cago Cubs to purchase the contracts of Junior Gilliam and Stubs Ferrell for $7,500 and $5,000 respectively. Gilliam and Ferrell reported on March 10 to the Cubs' Springfield, Massachusetts, club, which was in training in Haines City, Florida.[150]

The Cubs released both players three weeks later. "I hit over .300 during spring training and fielded well," a puzzled Gilliam told an in-terviewer. "To this day, I don't know what it was all about."[151] John T. Sheehan, president of the Cubs' minor league system, gave the Cubs' explanation of Gilliam's release in a March 31, 1950, letter to Powell: "Gilliam has been in training about three weeks and up until this time does not look as though he will be able to hit well enough to stay in this classification. If he does not improve his hitting it may be necessary for us to return him to you and we may do this before our season opens."[152]

Gilliam was also puzzled about Ferrell's release. In an undated letter to Powell, Gilliam wrote, "They gave him his release. They didn't give him much of a chance. He pitch in two games and one team beat him with a home run in the ninth. Another team hit four home runs off of him in three innings . . . the fence was 310 feet and the wind was blow-ing that way. All you had to do," Gilliam wrote in defense of his team-mate, "was hit it up in the air."[153] Powell wrote Ferrell a letter on March 30, 1950, saying in part, "Well, don't let it get you down Ferrell. You are young and still have a chance to try again at some time in the future."[154] Powell took both men back onto the Elites' squad, and he continued to encourage and promote their signing with organized baseball. On July 3, 1950, Powell sent handwritten letters to the Elmira (New York) Baseball

Club offering them Ferrell's contract for $2,500 and Gilliam's contract for $5,000.[155] Both men played for the Elites through 1950.

Westport Baseball Park was not completed in time for the start of the 1950 season, so the Elites opened—on Sunday, May 7, before 12,000 fans, 10,511 paid—at newly built Memorial Stadium. The stadium, built on the site of old Municipal Stadium, memorialized Baltimoreans killed in World War II. The turnout was the biggest crowd ever to see an Elites game in Baltimore, but the Park Board's rental fee severely diminished the Elites' proceeds. The Elites' bill came to more than $3,000. Had the Orioles drawn the same number of paying fans, their bill would have been $735.77, based on a rate of 7¢ a ticket.[156] Clearly, the Elites were charged at a much higher rate.

Following their opening day game, which they won, the Elites lost a Mother's Day doubleheader to the New York Cubans in the Polo Grounds the following weekend by the narrow margins of 2–1 and 7–6. Romby took the loss in game one. Wilmore had to relieve Black in the fifth inning of game two after the Cubans scored five runs.[157] The Elites played .500 ball for the rest of the first half, but attendance continued to fall. They split two doubleheaders with the Chicago American Giants. A local newspaper predicted 10,000 fans for one of the doubleheaders in Comiskey Park, but only 4,372 showed up.[158] In their first appearance in Baltimore after opening day, again at Memorial Stadium, as Westport was still not completed, the team attracted 4,400 fans—a far cry from the 12,000 on hand for opening day.[159]

By the end of June the Elites were in second place with a 5–6 league record behind the surprisingly strong Indianapolis Clowns at 17–13. The Clowns went on to win the Eastern Division first-half flag with a 29–17–1 record. The Elites held on to second place with a 10–9–1 finish.[160]

Westport was finally ready on July 2, for a Sunday doubleheader against the Giants from the Windy City. Conflicting notices about the starting time—one said 2 p.m. and one said it was to be a twi-night doubleheader—kept attendance to 1,500, but that did not faze the Elites. They came from behind in both games to sweep the twin bill 2–1 and 7–5. Wilmore won the opener, with the help of solid defense and a ninth inning double by rookie Fleming Reed to drive in Kimbro with the decisive tally. Joe Black won game two in relief of Leroy Ferrell. The Baltimoreans had a three-game winning streak going, for they had beaten Chicago the night before 10–3 in Wilmington, Delaware.[161]

The Kansas City Monarchs, who had won the first-half pennant in the Western Division, lost to the Elites 1–0 and 5–4 before a capacity, but nevertheless small, crowd of 2,000 spectators. Black's two-hit shutout in game one was described by a reporter as "a magnificently pitched game." Manager Lenny Pearson provided the Elites' only run, with a towering homer over the left field wall. Ferrell managed to make the most of five runs the Elites scored in game two. Gilliam's bases-loaded triple and theft of home were the game's highlights.[162]

The Elites lost one of their top hitters a week later when Pearson signed a contract with the Milwaukee Brewers in the American Association. Powell appointed Kimbro, the only remaining player from the 1938 Elite squad, to once again be the team's interim manager.

The team did well even without Pearson and posted a 14–11 record, good enough for first place. The Indianapolis Clowns finished the second half at 18–22–1,[163] but because none of the other Eastern Division teams, including the Elites, had played the required number of league games, the Clowns, who had played more than the required number of games, won the second-half pennant.[164] For both halves of the season, the Elites were in their familiar runner-up role.

The *Afro-American* continued its sparse coverage of the team. Much of the Negro league baseball news dealt with events away from Baltimore. Poor attendance forced the Louisville Buckeyes to fold after the first half of 1950. The Eagles, recently transposed from Newark to Houston, left Houston and played half of their 1950 games in Nashville. The New York Cubans found the financial strain too much to bear and folded in early 1951.[165]

With the Negro league financial picture dimming further, 1950 marked the beginning of the end for the Elites as a team but the opening of new vistas for several of its players. The team lost $18,000 and learned that organized baseball was courting three more of their number, Junior Gilliam, Joe Black, and Leroy "Stubs" Ferrell. For other Elites, 1950 marked the end of their Negro league career. Powell had released veterans Bill

Byrd and Leon Day two months into the season. Day signed with the Winnipeg Buffalos in the ManDak League in Manitoba, Canada, where Day's former Newark Eagle teammate, Willie Wells, was the manager.[166] Byrd became the player-manager for a team named the Negro League All Stars, an independent team based in Baltimore. Powell explained his decision to release the two players by saying that they were drawing salaries "far in excess of their rapidly declining market value."[167] Byrd's release meant Negro league baseball had lost its last legal spitballer.

Powell took a number of other steps in 1950 to bolster the team's diminishing finances. He ordered that games be stopped when a foul ball was hit into the stands to await the ball's return to the field.[168] He decided to pay his players a percentage of the gate in place of salary, starting with a Labor Day game against the Philadelphia Stars in which Satchel Paige, back from his major league tour with the Cleveland Indians, was on the mound for the Stars. Three other clubs, Houston, Birmingham, and Memphis, had been paying players on a percentage basis since June, but that did not carry any weight with Butts, Finney, John Coleman, and Wilmore. They refused to play. Powell suspended them indefinitely.[169]

The Labor Day game included Elites pitcher Hubert Simmons's one-time-at-bat against Paige. "I had to play right field," Simmons said, "because Alfred Henry, our right fielder, had to play shortstop in place of Butts. Kimbro moved in from center to play second in place of Finney. Paige pitched the first three innings. It was the first and only time I faced him. He was fast and could put the ball anywhere he wanted. The first pitch I just let go by. Next one I let go by for strike two. I was determined to swing at the third one, which I did but I missed it. He was something else."[170]

While Powell was seeking ways to improve the Elites' fortunes, officials of other Negro league clubs were coming up with a variety of ways to boost attendance. Most of the teams made money in 1949, but for three of the teams, Kansas City Monarchs, Chicago American Giants, and Birmingham Black Barons, the profits came not from ticket sales but from the sale of quality players to organized baseball, prompting J. B. Martin to argue that such sales would ensure the league's survival.[171] Martin overlooked the fact that the number of major league–caliber Negro league players was declining by 1950. Most promising young black players not already in the Negro leagues, like Maurice "Sonny" Wills, the pitching ace of Washington, D.C.'s Phelps High School team, were going straight to organized baseball's minor leagues. The Dodgers signed Wills after a baseball school tryout and placed him on a Class D Pony League team in Hornell, New York.[172] Better known as Maury Wills, he played eight years in the minors before embarking on a fourteen-year career with the Dodgers, Pirates, and Expos.

In view of the shortage of black players and hoping to boost attendance, Negro American League owners gave the Chicago American Giants permission to sign white players, though most thought it unlikely that whites would choose the Negro leagues over organized ball in great numbers.[173] The Chicago Giants signed three white players in July 1950—pitcher Louis Chirban, shortstop Frank Dyll, and second baseman Stanley Miarka. When asked if the three would be allowed to play in Birmingham and Memphis, where the stadiums had segregated seating, Martin said, "There isn't any law against them playing and if they don't play, I'll sue in federal court."[174]

White players in Chicago presented no problems. Chirban made his second appearance in a game against the Monarchs in Comiskey Park on July 16. He had to be lifted after giving up four hits and three runs in two innings. Dyll and Miarka made their first appearance in the eighth inning of the same game.[175] It was a different story in Birmingham, where there was a city ordinance against integrated teams. Public Safety Commissioner Bull Connor boarded the Chicago Giants' bus at the entrance to the Birmingham Black Barons' Rickwood Field and said, according to Butch McCord, then with the Chicago Giants, "I hear you got some white players on this team. If you put them on the field I'm going to close the ballpark down." "Well," McCord continued, "we had to do what he said, so our white players watched the game in the white section of the segregated stands."[176] "I didn't know who he was," McCord added, "until I saw him on TV in the '60s turning the dogs loose on those people."[177] Giants' management considered filing a suit but decided against it.[178] None of the three white players played for a Negro league team in 1951.

This was not the first time a white man had played on a Negro league team. The Cleveland Buckeyes had signed pitcher Eddie Klep for the 1946 season, but Jim Crow laws also prevented Klep from playing with the team in parts of the South.[179] He pitched three innings against the Atlanta Black Crackers without incident in Atlanta, Georgia, but met the same fate as did the three white Chicago American Giants in Birmingham. Upon learning that Klep was white, Bull Connor told Buckeyes press secretary Jimmy Jones, "Get him outta here and quick. We don't have no mixing down here." Jones complied, and Klep watched the game from the "white" section of the stadium. The Buckeyes released Klep in the spring of 1947.[180]

In another instance of reverse integration, a white player took the field with the Elites for an exhibition game in the spring of 1945 at Bugle Field, but he was playing as a stopgap measure, not to generate ticket sales. Bobby Holmes, a high school player for Baltimore Polytechnic Institute, impressed several of the Elites as he was taking batting practice with his team on the field before the Elites' game. The Elites needed a shortstop that day, and Holmes happily obliged. He helped turn two double plays and stroked two hits.[181]

The only bright financial spots for Richard Powell in 1950 were options the Dodgers offered in December for the right to sign Gilliam and Black, but they provided no immediate cash. Should the Dodgers decide to sign the two players, the Elites would not be paid until the contracts were signed, which would not happen until after spring training in 1951, when the Dodgers made the final decisions. Powell considered dismantling the Elites but knew that if he did, the Dodgers would not have to pay him for Gilliam and Black, because neither player would be under contract. So he took the team to Charlotte, North Carolina, for spring training for what he knew would be a short 1951 season in Baltimore.

Why Powell again chose Charlotte for spring training is not known, but he did receive an invitation from Edward C. Bush, owner of the New Queen City Hotel in Columbus, Mississippi, to conduct spring training there. Bush's offer to Powell is an example of arrangements that players could expect at black hotels in the South at the time. Two players would share a room for 1 dollar per man per day including "shower bath and tub." Meals were 60 cents each including drinks. A typical breakfast would be two eggs, bacon or sausage or ham, and grits. Players would have a choice of one meat and three vegetables for dinner, the noon meal. Supper would feature liver and rice, or pork chops and rice, with one vegetable "or anything special that the individual might prefer."[182]

As Powell knew it would, the Dodgers' check for Gilliam and Black arrived in April 1951. There are conflicting reports on the amount of the check. According to former Dodgers' official Mickey McConnell in an interview with Hall of Fame sportswriter Red Smith, the Dodgers got both players for $5,500. Branch Rickey offered Powell $4,000 for Gilliam. Powell reportedly countered by asking for $5,000 because he needed funds "to pay some bills and buy a new bus." Powell also offered to include Black in the $5,000 offer. Rickey countered by re-offering $4,000 for Gilliam and adding $500 "to look at Black," with the understanding that Rickey would pay Powell another $1,000 if the Dodgers kept Black.[183] The final figure was $10,000, $5,000 apiece. In an April 16, 1951, letter from Montreal Royals' general manager, G. Moreau, to Powell, Moreau said he was enclosing a $10,000 check representing final payment for Gilliam ($5,000) and Black ($5,000). Earlier, in a December 12, 1950, letter, Moreau had sent $1,500 to cover the option to purchase both players' contracts. Both were assigned to the Montreal Royals.

The Dodgers had also invited Ferrell to spring training and he had attended, but they did not sign him. Frazier Robinson said, "Ferrell had a chance in spring training with the Dodgers but couldn't push himself away from the dinner table."[184]

Joe Black joined the Dodgers in 1952. He won Rookie of the Year honors and became the first African American to win a World Series game when the Dodgers beat the Yankees, 4–2, in game one of the 1952 World Series at Ebbets Field. Gilliam joined Black on the Dodgers' roster in early 1953 and succeeded him as Rookie of the Year.

Around the same time Powell received the Dodgers' final check, he received an offer to buy the whole team "for just under $10,000" from a wealthy black nightclub owner in Nashville, Sou Bridgeforth.[185] Powell wanted to keep the team in Baltimore and had been negotiating a possible sale with white Howard Street restaurateur Leonard Green, but those negotiations broke down.[186] After fourteen years in the Monumental City, the Elites moved back to the city where they started, leaving Baltimoreans without a Negro league team.[187] On the team that returned to Nashville, only Kimbro remained from the 1938 team that had gone to Baltimore. Hard-hitting outfielder Jim Zapp, who played briefly with the Elites in 1946, was back in the outfield. Hoss Walker was again the team's manager.

With only a handful of experienced players, the now Nashville Elite Giants struggled. They played anywhere they could schedule a game, which included Buffalo, New York, Chicago, and Memphis, with only an occasional stop in Baltimore. During the last week of May, the Elites and the now New Orleans Eagles, recently of Nashville and Houston, hooked up for games across Louisiana—in New Orleans, Monroe, Houma, Opelousas, and Alexandria—as well as in Natchez, Mississippi.[188]

The traveling took its toll. Near the middle of the 1951 season the team was at 0–10.[189] According to one report in July, the Elites began winning some games, "making a strong bid for the number-one spot in the second-half drive."[190] While they did not attain the number-one spot, the Elites did finish the second half with a 15–12 record, but their 13–24 record for the first half put them in third place for the season, out of the three remaining teams in the NAL East.[191] The team's finances were exhausted. The team folded at the end of the season.

Richard Powell, who remained in Baltimore, wanted to stay in baseball. He offered to scout for the team that had signed three of his players. Fresco Thompson, a Dodgers vice-president, said in a May 25, 1951, letter to Powell, that the Dodgers were not hiring any new scouts because, "so many young prospects for organized baseball are entering military service that I am having considerable difficulty in keeping my present scouting staff busy."[192] Powell applied unsuccessfully to other clubs for a scouting position. The Chicago Cubs' director of player personnel told him in an April 25, 1952, letter, "Our scouting budget is over subscribed and it will be impossible for us to take on additional scouts."[193] Mickey Shader, chief scout for the San Francisco Seals, of the Pacific Coast League, informed Powell in a March 21, 1952, letter, "We are not branching out so far from home, so consequently we are not in a position to hire another scout as our scouting staff is now full."[194] Powell took a job with the Social Security Administration, where he worked for the next twenty years.[195] He had married Henryene Green in 1951, but the marriage ended in divorce. Powell spent his last years in Baltimore's Basilica Place Apartments, across the street from the Enoch Pratt Library.[196]

Baltimore's only professional baseball team now was the International League Baltimore Orioles. That would change in 1954.

EPILOGUE

Integration, Disintegration

T he American League St. Louis Browns came to town in April of 1954 and took the name Baltimore Orioles, which the International League Orioles no longer needed, because they moved to Richmond, Virginia. In February of that year, the team released Satchel Paige, who had pitched for the Browns from 1951 to 1953. Paige returned to barnstorming. Another pitcher, thirty-four-year-old Jehosie "Jay" Heard, started the season as the major league Orioles' first black player, but he was sent to the minors in June after pitching only three and a third innings. Joseph Vann Durham was Baltimore's second African American player. Joe Durham also had a limited tenure, playing in the outfield for ten games at the end of the '54 season.[1]

The push for equal rights continued in Baltimore during the new Orioles' maiden season. Baltimore city's public school system became the first south of the Mason-Dixon Line to integrate. The Board of Education voted to do so just months after Thurgood Marshall, a Baltimorean, prevailed in the Supreme Court's *Brown v. Board of Education* decision on May 17, 1954.[2] Vic Power, a black player for the International League Syracuse Chiefs who went on to a twelve-year major league career, appeared in a four-game series against the IL Orioles in Baltimore in September of 1951 without any incident such as the one that occurred in front of the Royals' locker room when Jackie Robinson made his first Baltimore appearance as a Royal in 1946.[3] Some white fans still let loose with a barrage of unflattering names directed toward visiting black play-

134

ers. Junior Gilliam, as a member of the Montreal Royals, played in Memorial Stadium in 1951 and 1952. "The fans," Gilliam said, "got on me. But, hearing those names I just bore down harder."[4]

The Maryland Commission on Interracial Problems and Relations gave Governor Theodore McKeldin both good and bad news on the state of race relations in Maryland in 1954. The Lyric Theater had reversed itself and allowed contralto Marian Anderson to perform there, ending its practice of excluding black performers. The Baltimore City Fire Department had hired twenty-two African Americans. Most department stores accepted black customers and two large chains of variety shops had ended discrimination at their food counters. All major Baltimore hotels served food to African American groups that conducted business in the hotel but did not allow them to stay in the hotels.[5] The commission found "sharply divided problems in such areas as employment, recreation, hotel, restaurant, and movie facilities; health education, and full recognition of the Negro as a first-class citizen."[6]

Those problems prompted Walter White, secretary of the NAACP in New York City, to wire Will Harridge, president of the American League, on September 25, 1953, asking Harridge to block the pending transfer of the St. Louis Browns to Baltimore. The telegram said in part, "Because of the city's rigid pattern of segregation, including the exclusion of Negroes from hotels and restaurants, the NAACP urges the American League not to approve transfer of franchise of St. Louis baseball team to city of Baltimore."[7] The transfer went forth nevertheless, and Baltimore welcomed their new team with a gala parade on the Orioles' home opening day, April 15, 1954. More than 350,000 people turned out to see the players, who tossed plastic baseballs to the crowd from an eleven-car procession that included floats featuring Miss and Mrs. Marylands dressed in bathing suits and furs. The O's beat the White Sox 3–1 behind the pitching of Bob Turley.[8]

Hoping to enlist baseball's support once the team was in town, Roy Wilkins, administrator of the NAACP in New York, wrote Harridge on April 9, 1954, asking him to "use such persuasion as your office has at its disposal . . . to insist on hotel and restaurant facilities for their entire teams regardless of race or color." Wilkins pointed out that Baltimore was the only American League city to bar blacks from white-owned hotels and restaurants. Appealing to baseball's economic interests, Wilkins wrote, "The matter is not a 'social problem,' outside the interest and activity of baseball officials, but one that involves 'squad morale.'" Clubs with Negro players could be penalized unfairly, Wilkins pointed out, which could "conceivably, in a close race, affect team standings and the financial rewards of players and owners."[9] Harridge's response has not been found. Governor McKeldin made the same request of Baltimore hotel operators at a meeting with them on April 7, 1954. They refused. The operators' attorney, Charles D. Harris, said, "The hotel men are in business to make a profit, and they stand to lose if they go ahead of public opinion."[10] It was not until 1957 that the Baltimore Hotel Association decided that "colored members of college and professional athletic teams" could stay in their hotels.[11]

Baltimore would see the remnants of segregation removed by the federal civil rights legislation of the 1960s and 1970s. Two members of Old West's politically prominent Mitchell family took an active role in that legislative activity. Parren Mitchell went to Washington as Maryland's first black congressman. A Democrat, he represented Maryland's 7th Congressional District from 1971 to 1987. Parren's older brother, Clarence Mitchell Jr., as chief lobbyist for the NAACP for thirty years, was at the forefront of the federal civil rights legislation of the '60s and '70s. Often called the "101st senator," Clarence Mitchell was memorialized by Baltimore, which named its main courthouse after him shortly after his death in 1984.[12]

Victorine Adams became the first woman and the first African American woman to win election to the Baltimore City Council when she was elected in 1968 from the 4th District in Northeast Baltimore. Four white women had previously served on the council but each had been appointed, to finish her husband's term.[13] Mrs. Adams had run unsuccessfully in 1962 for the state Senate. Four years later she won election to the House of Delegates, but she resigned after a year to run for the City Council. She held her council seat for four terms, until 1983.[14]

Discrimination would ease but not disappear in Baltimore and in the major leagues. The fight for equal rights on America's professional baseball diamonds was far from over, but a start had been made. Three of the major leagues' black pioneers—Roy Campanella, Joe Black, and James "Junior" Gilliam—got their start with the Baltimore Elite Giants.

By the time one of those pioneers, Joe Black, threw his World Series shutout against the Yankees, the Negro leagues were in irreversible decline. Integration of the majors, which black fans, players, owners, and sportswriters had advocated for decades, continued but it diverted black fans from Negro league parks to major league parks. The diversion did not come as a surprise. In August of 1942, Washington-Homestead Grays manager Vic Harris proposed that integration of baseball take a different course: the Negro leagues should build up their teams to the point where they could compete successfully with the major league teams rather than integrate the majors with individual players. "If they take our best boys," Harris said, "we will be but a hollow shell of what we are today."[15] Harris's words proved prophetic. Many who were close to the Negro leagues found its demise painful. The institution they loved was dying, and they were powerless to do anything about it. Some took black fans to task for what they saw as a lack of loyalty to the Negro leagues. Butch McCord thought fans should have kept going to Negro league games to show that "we're just as good as the white leagues." "Instead," he said, "black fans started going to see Jackie, first in International League cities in 1946 and in National League cities in 1947 and beyond. You had black fans riding segregated trains, eating segregated sandwiches, and staying in segregated hotels. They sat in the bleachers 'cause they couldn't sit in the stands."[16]

Effa Manley found many people to blame, most of them black. In September of 1948, shortly before she and Abe sold the Eagles, she said, "Negro fans are acting like damn fools." Citing the same reasoning as McCord, she went on to say, "Negro fans have deserted the Negro teams because a few players get four cents more and the white teams have put their stamp of approval on them." She also blamed the black press for not educating fans about their responsibility to the Negro leagues. The fans' reactions and the press's lack of action were, for her, expressions of Negroes' inferiority complex. By her reckoning, black players who went to the majors were setting themselves up for a fall; she was sure that concerns about social equality would keep white teams "from using Negroes consistently." Many Negroes in the minor leagues were unhappy, Effa observed, and four had quit. In her opinion, owners of white teams did not want to see black players be the target of approval and adulation, especially from white women; she predicted that three hundred people would lose their jobs if the Negro leagues folded.[17]

However, for the black fans who were going to the major league parks, Jackie Robinson and other blacks in the majors offered a beacon of progress, hope, and pride. Mike Royko of the *Chicago Daily News* captured blacks' pride in his description of the scene at Wrigley Field when the 1947 Dodgers made their first trip to Chicago. Royko, a white man, wrote of blacks, "coming by the thousands, pouring off the northbound Els and out of their cars. They didn't wear baseball game clothes. They had on church clothes and funeral clothes: suits, white shirts, ties, gleaming shoes, and straw hats. A tall, middle-aged black man that sat next to me had a smile of almost painful joy on his face. He beat his palms together so hard they must have hurt."[18] The blacks' wardrobe had its impact on Royko who did not know that blacks always wore "church clothes and funeral clothes" to their baseball games. Two years later, hundreds of people in Baltimore stopped work up and down Pennsylvania Avenue for two hours on October 7 to listen to and watch accounts of Robinson's play with the Dodgers during the third game of the 1949 World Series against the Yankees. Pool halls without a radio or television were vacant. A crowd of two hundred gathered in front of a store at 1300 Pennsylvania Avenue where a television set broadcast the game. Another one hundred people, including entertainer Redd Foxx, crowded into a darkened pool room to sit on chairs and pool tables to watch the game.[19]

As black players moved into organized baseball, black doctors, teachers, lawyers, dentists, morticians, entrepreneurs, and entertainers moved to the suburbs. They left behind the remains of what had once been a vibrant way of life. Fewer black teenage boys had a shot at pro ball as organized baseball started taking only the very best. The reservoir of coaching and executive abilities represented by Richard Powell, Biz Mackey, Vic Harris, George Scales, and Felton Snow went untapped. Old West unraveled. The York Hotel has long since disappeared. The Shake 'n' Bake

Family Fun Center stands near where the Regent Theater once did. Public housing stands on sites once occupied by restaurants and clubs. A statue of jazz singer Billie Holiday, a Baltimore native, sits diagonally across Pennsylvania Avenue from where the Royal Theater once stood, to remind passersby of the neighborhood's musical history. It is hard to see much excitement in the faces of those who tread Pennsylvania Avenue today. Old West neighborhoods are still largely black, but the residents no longer have access to the best teachers and doctors.

Democratization of the national pastime came too late for most Baltimore Elite Giants. Being excluded from the majors was a bitter pill for some, while others accepted the color bar as a fact of life. Henry Kimbro, who played with the Elites for more years than anyone else, took the latter stance. "I really didn't think the game would ever be integrated," Kimbro said. "You had some people in baseball who controlled it, and they weren't for integration at all. Trying to look ahead at baseball being integrated then was like trying to look through a mountain. We weren't close enough to the top then that we could look in the distance and see the other side."[20] Kimbro noted that the constant travel and barnstorming demanded a lot of the players, but, he mused, "we were young back then. Young and getting paid to play baseball. Who cared how far we had to ride? We were on top of the world."[21]

For James "Red" Moore, who played first base for the Elites in 1939–40, playing in the Negro leagues "was the greatest thing that ever happened to me." At age 10 he played stickball with friends, listened to major league games on the radio, and asked his parents, "Why aren't some of us in the league?" His parents told him that Negroes "couldn't play with the white teams." Moore learned about the Negro leagues from articles in the *Atlanta World*, which printed news of the black teams. Then, says Moore, "my ambition became to play in the Negro leagues." He realized his ambition when he made the Atlanta Black Crackers team in 1935. "We didn't make too much," he remembered, "but we traveled around and made some money. My dad liked to be talking about his son."[22]

Leon Day also looked back without regret: "We were a good bunch of guys traveling down the highway. One guy would start telling lies; then another and another. Then we'd start singing 'Sweet Adeline.' Play cards sometimes. Play some rummy. Get to the ballpark, play the game, and get right back on the bus."[23]

According to Richard Powell, many of the descriptions of the poor conditions that confronted players were overblown: "Hell, we played on major league fields all across the country . . . and as for not getting served in restaurants, that applied to all coloreds, not just ball players . . . They [players] were riding buses but were going to cities they'd never seen before and the buses were taking them to play ball. Baseball was all that mattered.[24]

Others were angry. Butch McCord, who played minor league ball from 1951 to 1961 (when he often hit over .300 and was twice honored as the best first baseman in the American Association, winning the association's Silver Glove Award in 1956 and 1958), had some not-so-fond memories: "We were in the slave market back then. We couldn't go anywhere else because there was nowhere else to go. If we wanted to play baseball, we had to play when and where the owners told us to play."[25] On another occasion McCord said, "It took 15 years to get over the hurt of not making it to the majors."[26]

Joe Black had bitter memories of the treatment he received from the majors before he signed with the Dodgers: "The scouts wouldn't, didn't talk to me. They said 'colored guys don't play baseball.' . . . I hated white people. I couldn't understand it. I'm an American and I couldn't play baseball, the No. 1 pastime."[27] The Dodgers' failure to return to him two clippings he had sent to the Dodgers' Bob Finch in 1947 did not make him feel any better toward whites. Black enclosed the clippings in a letter describing his accomplishments, including a win over the Saint Paul Saints of the American Association, the subject of the clippings. He ended his letter with, "Please return these clippings as they belong to my wife's scrapbook." The clippings remained in the Dodgers' files until December of 1952 when the Dodgers finally returned them to Black.[28]

Biz Mackey rued the money that might have been. In a 1954 interview he said, "The fact that I'm not around now that Negro ballplayers are getting a break bothers me no little. Think of the salary I, along with a lot of other colored guys might have made with the hustle which was

Silver Glove awarded to Clinton "Butch" McCord

typical of our time."[29] Mackey made $375 a month, or about $2,250 for the season, with the Newark Eagles in 1946–47.[30] Junior Gilliam signed with the Dodgers in 1954 for $10,000 a year.[31]

As the teams folded, the only people from the Negro leagues making money were the players with organized baseball, where all executives, managers, coaches, and support staff were white. This point was not lost on Audley "Queen Mother" Moore, a civil rights and political rights activist whose influence was felt throughout the world from her home base in Harlem. As she put it,

When our teams played in the communities throughout our country, our communities were ablaze with activity—our hotels, we had hotels and all, we used to have taxis, shoeshine boys, old women selling candies and peanuts and everything. Our youngsters had something to aspire to. There were activities, right? Well, honey, now you have a Negro, or ten Negroes or twenty Negroes there [the majors], but the white man gets all the gate; he gets all the receipts, the profits.[32]

The Baltimore Elite Giants and the other Negro league teams are history, but former players and others have kept the memories of the teams alive. Starting in the late 1960s, former players held reunions, spoke to school and community groups, gave interviews to the news and entertainment media, and attended baseball card shows where they signed autographs and swapped stories about games and friends gone by. Such talks and gatherings will soon be a memory. Former players continue to be active, but they are getting older and are finding it more difficult to travel. Stanley Glenn said in 2006, "There are only twenty-five of us left, men who played in the leagues before 1951."[33]

One of them, Bert Simmons, reports that his "best feeling in baseball" came in 2003 while he was speaking about his career to a group of fourth graders at Govans Elementary School in Baltimore.

The class wrote to the Baltimore Orioles asking me to throw out the first pitch in a June game at Camden Yards. The O's called. I told 'em "I'd love to, but you have to let the kids come." They agreed and they sent buses to get the kids and their parents. They escorted me to the field, down the ramp. The kids were yelling. The jumbo screen showed me on the mound. A lady handed me the ball. I took my windup and threw a strike. I didn't want to bounce the ball up to the plate so I had practiced. I went back to the school in the fall to thank the kids.[34]

Simmons was the subject of another honor when the church to which he belongs, Lochearn Presbyterian at 3800 Patterson Avenue in Baltimore, recognized his career in the Negro leagues and his subsequent baseball activities in Baltimore with a special day for him on February 18, 2007, as part of the church's observance of Black History Month. Several of the children who wrote the letters to the Orioles and their teacher attended.

Writers have taken an interest in the Negro leagues. Robert Peterson's classic 1970 book, *Only the Ball Was White*, marked the first published, in-depth treatment of the Negro leagues. Peterson, who was white, had played against many Negro teams in his youth and thought the time had come to recount the accomplishments of top-echelon Negro baseball players. Today, the reader can choose from well over one hundred books on the Negro leagues.

Four Baltimore Little League teams—two in Bolton Hill and two in Govans—played their 1993 season in replica uniforms of the Elites and the Baltimore Black Sox. The Children of Lenore P. and Harvey M. Meyerhoff Philanthropic Fund of the Associated Jewish Community Federation selected the teams based on proposals received from a number of teams. The federation gave a $15,000 grant for uniforms and equipment. Robert Hieronimus and his wife Zohara, Baltimore radio personalities, came up with the idea. Hieronimus recalls going to Negro league games with his father, being dismayed at the conditions under which they played, and admiring the players' lack of complaint. Negro league baseball, especially in Baltimore, is a piece of history Hieronimus wants to preserve. Former Negro leaguers Stanley Glenn and Bill "Ready" Cash of the Stars and Wilmer Fields of the Washington-Homestead Grays were on hand when the uniforms were presented and shared stories of their days in the real flannels.[35]

The five-team minor division of the Wilmington, Delaware, Little League opened its 2006 season with players wearing "retro replica stylings" of uniforms of five Negro league teams—the Wilmington/Washington Potomacs, Kansas City Monarchs, Homestead Grays, Pittsburgh Crawfords, and the Elites. Wilmington Little League president Clark Lewis thought of the idea when he heard about the induction of seventeen Negro leaguers into the Hall of Fame scheduled for July of 2006. Lewis reported that the idea was well received and that the 8–10-year-old players "learned about a segregated era of baseball they didn't know existed."[36]

Major league players have worn the Elites' uniform. The Baltimore Orioles donned uniforms similar to those of the Elites and the Detroit Tigers wore replicas of the Detroit Stars' uniform for a night game on July 5, 1997, in Camden Yards. The Orioles flew in Don Troy, who pitched for the Elites in 1944 and 1945, and Rosa Parks, who sparked the bus boycott in Montgomery, Alabama, by refusing to sit in the back of the bus, for the festivities.[37]

Memories of the Elites can also be found at The Sports Legends

Museum at Camden Yards. There the visitor will find memorabilia that include a mock-up of the team bus, signed baseballs, photographs, and a model of Bugle Field. The Cal Ripken Museum in Aberdeen, Maryland, features a tribute to Ernest Burke, a native of nearby Perryville, who pitched for the Elites and played in the minors.

A permanent memorial to the Baltimore Elite Giants would ensure that their days in Baltimore are remembered. Why not build a facsimile of Bugle Field large enough to show fans in the stands and players in Elite uniforms on the field? Placed at an entrance to Camden Yards, it would remind fans of all ages and hues that Baltimore once was home to one of the top teams in the Negro leagues.

ACKNOWLEDGMENTS

Now that I am retired, in the sense that I voluntarily left the world of employment after a forty-year career in human resource development, I can pursue my hobby of writing baseball history on a full-time basis. The more I write, the more I meet people who share my interest in the game and who give generously of their time, expertise, support, and experience.

Robert J. Brugger, history editor at the Johns Hopkins University Press, saw more in the initial manuscript than I did. His suggestions about what he referred to as the "architecture of the book" and his patience with a writer aspiring to be a historian added needed depth and clarity to the book. Thank you, Bob. Thanks also to Josh Tong, acquisitions assistant at the Johns Hopkins University Press, for his guidance on preparing photographs for the book. Dave Almy of Garrett Park, Maryland, an architect by profession and an avid baseball fan, lent his professional talent to the book by drawing the picture of Bugle Field that appears in the book.

Paul Dickson, the author of fifty-two books and counting, has been a steadfast source of encouragement and advice in matters ranging from writing and research techniques to working with publishers, agents, and bookstores. Thank you, Paul. Brad Snyder, author of two major baseball books, read an early draft and delivered a boatload of helpful feedback. Brad, I hope you see your fingerprints in the final product. Thomas Cripps, University Distinguished Professor (retired) at Morgan State University in Baltimore, provided many helpful suggestions on researching the racial and community aspects of the book. James Bready, the author of two books on baseball in Baltimore, offered many helpful suggestions about the book's content.

I find it exciting to follow the trail of a story as one bit of information leads to more questions, whose answers lie in the documents found in libraries, collections, and archives and in the memories of people with first-hand experience.

Barbara Powell "Babs" Golden graciously gave me access to the papers of her father, Richard Powell, where I found original letters, telegrams, and photographs that are available nowhere else. Ronald A. Rooks helped me go through the papers and shared his recollections of Mayor McKeldin.

The staff at the Library of Congress has been unfailingly helpful and courteous. In particular I am indebted to Dave Kelly for his insightful and prompt response to questions; to Sibyl Moses, the library's African American specialist, and to the staff of the library's Manuscript Division and the Newspaper and Current Periodical Reading Room. People at the Manuscript Division of the Moorland Spingarn Research Center at Howard University gave me easy access to Art Carter's papers. I found much information on Tom Wilson and the early days of the Elite Giants in Nashville's Metropolitan Archives. Ken Fieth made the arrangements for my work there. Linda Center spent a day with me showing me documents I would never have found on my own. The staff at the Baltimore City Archives helped me sort through Mayor Theodore McKeldin's papers to find what I needed, as did the staff in the Maryland Room at the University of Maryland's Hornbake Library. Thomas Saunders gave me a guided tour of Old West and described the high points of life along Pennsylvania Avenue. Fred Shoken unearthed some hard-to-find information on who owned Bugle Field. Bill Sleeman at the Thurgood Marshall Library in Baltimore provided access to Vernon Green's papers. Members of the research staff at Baseball's Hall of Fame in Cooperstown, New York—Jim Gates, Claudette Burke, Freddy Berowski, and Pat Kelly—made my time there productive and pleasant. Robert Hieronimus, known as "Dr. Bob" to Elite Giants fans throughout Baltimore, explained the many efforts he and his wife, Zohara, have taken to support keeping the Elites' story alive. Jeff Korman, manager of the Maryland Department at Baltimore's Enoch Pratt Free Library, provided photographs and information on the library's history with regard to segregation.

One of my great joys was talking with people who lived the history I was writing. Clinton "Butch" McCord offered many stories of his days in the Negro leagues and invited me to accompany him to two games of the Nashville Sounds—a pleasant way to do research. James "Red" Moore recalled the major events of his years with several Negro league teams, including the Elites. Stanley Glenn filled me in on the social importance of Negro league baseball by teaching me about the "Happening." Monte Irvin described his days playing at Bugle Field and how to strike out Roy Campanella. Clarence "Shad" Brown spent several hours talking about his career in Baltimore and his memories of Elites games. Baltimore natives Frederick Lonesome and Irving Morris told me what it was like to attend games at Bugle Field and to grow up in a segregated Old West. Helene King made it possible for me to interview both gentlemen at the Levindale Hebrew Geriatric Center in Baltimore. George Henderson, Paul Bonomo, and Jim O'Connor invited me to a meeting of their Baltimore Old-Timers' Baseball Club, where I heard first-hand stories from several members who had played at Bugle Field and attended games there. Charlotte Harvey told me about her life with Elites pitcher Bill Harvey and provided several photographs.

Robert "Skip" McAfee, a member of the Bibliography Committee of the Society for American Baseball Research, did a thorough job of preparing the index. Anne M. Whitmore, a senior manuscript editor at the Hopkins Press, did the painstaking and important copyediting work. Kathy Alexander, publicity manager at the Hopkins Press, conceived and carried out a far-reaching marketing plan for the book.

My wife, Judy Wentworth, has given generously of support and encouragement, as have former colleagues, Michael Berney, Jim Buchanan, Phyllis Drum, and Kate Lynott.

I am grateful for the contributions made by one and all. Any errors are mine alone.

The Elites were neither Baltimore's first black professional team nor its first Negro league team. The Lord Hannibals and the Orientals were the first organized, paid black teams in Baltimore and played their first game at Newington Park in 1874.[1] Both teams were short lived. Another team, the Lord Baltimores, played briefly in 1887. The Norfolk Elites, owned by lightweight boxing champion and Baltimore native Joe "Old Master" Gans, operated for a few years around the beginning of the twentieth century.[2]

The Baltimore Stars played during the Great Depression and had two future Hall of Famers on their roster: Ben Taylor, who owned the team and was the best Negro league first baseman of his time, and his successor as the Negro league's best first baseman, Buck Leonard. Leonard played for the Stars in 1933 before joining the Homestead Grays. The Baltimore Stars played their home games at Druid Hill Park, an open area with no fences, where three to five thousand fans sat on the grass and contributed a total of twenty to thirty dollars as the hat was passed. To help make ends meet, Leonard, his brother Charlie, and three other players stayed at Taylor's house at 1315 Madison Avenue. A seven-passenger Buick and a 1929 Ford with a rumble seat carried the team to games throughout North Carolina, West Virginia, and Pennsylvania.[3]

The city's first team to be part of a Negro league,[4] the Baltimore Black Sox, played at Maryland Park, near the intersection of Bush and Russell Streets, from 1916 to 1932. The *Baltimore Afro-American* described Maryland Park as "a sewer . . . which featured broken seats, holes in the roof, nonworking toilets, and weeds on the field."[5] Fans brought liquor to the games and shared it with the players.[6] The team entered into its first Negro league affiliation when it joined the Eastern Colored League in 1923. The ECL folded, due to financial losses, in November 1928. The Black Sox played as an independent team in 1928. The Black Sox reached their

The 1929 American Negro League Champion Baltimore Black Sox. Standing, left to right: *Robert Clarke, Willis Flournoy, Holsey Lee, Oliver Marcelle, Jesse Hubbard, Merven Ryan, Peter Washington, William Force.* Seated, left to right: *Herbert Dixon, James Cooke, Domingo Gomez, Frank Warfield, Jud Wilson, Dick Lundy, and Laymon Yokeley.*

high point in 1929, when they won the pennant of the newly formed American Negro League.[7] The league disbanded for the 1930 season but emerged for one final year, 1931, with the Black Sox as a member. The Sox played again as an independent team in 1932 before joining the resurgent Negro National League in 1933.

The Black Sox operated under the successive ownerships of four white businessmen. Charles P. Spedden was a clerk for the Baltimore and Ohio Railroad office before deciding to devote all of his time to baseball.[8] Spedden sold the team in the 1920s to restaurant owner George S. Rossiter, who entertained politicians at his speakeasy at 1001 S. Hanover Street, a little more than a mile from Maryland Park, and at the ballpark.[9] The Great Depression forced Rossiter to sell the team in 1932 to another white Baltimore businessman, Joe Cambria.[10] Cambria installed the Black Sox at 1500 Edison Boulevard (less than a mile from his supply company) and named the park Bugle Field after his company, the Bugle Coat, Apron and Towel Supply Company, at 1501–1507 North Chester Street.[11] Cambria, and his wife, Charlotte, lived six miles to the west, near Gwynns Falls Park, at 3403 Alto Road. The Depression and his refusal to pay competitive salaries left Cambria with no better luck than Rossiter had had. The top players went elsewhere.

By late June of 1934, Jack Farrell, a promoter from Chester, Pennsylvania, had bought the Black Sox from Cambria.[12] The team opened the 1934 season at Bugle Field by beating Tom Wilson's Nashville Elite Giants. After the game, the Sox left for an extended western trip. A dispute arose between the Philadelphia Stars' owner, Ed Bolden, and the Pittsburgh Crawfords' owner, Gus Greenlee, about scheduling league games in Baltimore. Bolden had opposed letting the Black Sox join the Negro National League, even though they had been voted in the previous year, because he considered Baltimore a poor baseball town.[13] Bolden's view prevailed. The Black Sox never played another game in Baltimore.

The team counted two eventual Hall of Famers among their members in the early 1930s. The first was Satchel Paige, who pitched for the team in 1930 and went on to become the best-known Negro league player of all time. In 1971, "Satch" became the first Negro leaguer inducted into the Hall of Fame. The second Hall of Famer was right-handed fireballer Leon Day. Day, who grew up in Baltimore's Mount Winans neighborhood in South Baltimore along the Baltimore and Ohio Railroad tracks, made his debut with Baltimore's semi-pro Silver Moon baseball club in 1934 and joined the Black Sox as a second baseman midway through the season.[14] Day made his mark on the game as a pitcher for the Newark Eagles, but he also hit with authority and played every position except catcher. He was inducted into the Hall of Fame in 1993.

Baltimore experienced a period of three years without a professional black baseball team, until the Elite Giants arrived in 1938.

APPENDIX B. BALTIMORE ELITE GIANTS BASEBALL CLUB OPERATING STATEMENT, 1947

Gross receipts—home games	$36,693.93
Gross receipts—away games	26,213.72
Total receipts	$62,907.65

Expenses

Salaries	$37,444.17
Transportation	2,788.26
Hotel & meals	7,689.87
Bus expenses	2,324.67
Baseball equipment	4,266.96
Advertising	1,165.29
League fees	1,750.00
Office supplies	738.29
Insurance	949.48
Social Security tax	373.44
Unemployment compensation tax	1,010.99
Miscellaneous	2,125.44
Telephone & Telegraph	355.08
Depreciation (bus)	1,835.00

Total expenses	$64,816.94
Net loss for year	$1,909.29

Source: Legal Papers of Dallas Nicholas and William Gosnell. Vernon Green Estate. Thurgood Marshall Law Library. Baltimore, MD. Box 10A1a: 1940–1969.

APPENDIX C. BALTIMORE ELITE GIANTS
STANDINGS, 1938–1951

Negro league records are incomplete and in some cases inconsistent. The information below is the most comprehensive available as of this writing. Further research may yield different results.

Negro National League

1938	1st Half Only
Homestead Grays	26–6
Philadelphia Stars	20–11
Pittsburgh Crawfords	14–14
Newark Eagles	11–11
Baltimore Elite Giants	**12–14**
New York Black Yankees	4–17
Washington Black Senators	1–20

1939	Totals
Homestead Grays	33–14
Newark Eagles	29–20
Baltimore Elite Giants	**25–21**
Philadelphia Stars	31–32
New York Black Yankees	15–21
New York Cubans	5–22

1940	Totals
Homestead Grays	28–13
Baltimore Elite Giants	**25–14**
Newark Eagles	25–17
New York Cubans	12–19
Philadelphia Stars	16–31
New York Black Yankees	10–22

1941	1st Half	2nd Half
Homestead Grays	17–9	8–8
Newark Eagles	11–6	8–5
Baltimore Elite Giants	**13–10**	**9–8**
New York Cubans	7–10	4–2
New York Black Yankees	7–13	5–5
Philadelphia Stars	10–18	2–8

1942	Totals
Baltimore Elite Giants	**37–15**
Homestead Grays	26–17
Philadelphia Stars	21–17
Newark Eagles	19–17
New York Black Yankees	7–19
New York Cubans	6–19

1943	Totals
Homestead Grays	31–9
New York Cubans	20–9
Newark Eagles	19–14
Philadelphia Stars	21–18
Baltimore Elite Giants	**17–24**
New York Black Yankees	2–21

1944	1st Half	2nd Half
Homestead Grays	15–8	12–4
Baltimore Elite Giants	**12–11**	**12–9**
New York Cubans	12–10	4–4
Philadelphia Stars	7–11	12–7
Newark Eagles	13–9	6–13
New York Black Yankees	2–13	2–11

1945	1st Half	2nd Half
Homestead Grays	18–7	14–6
Philadelphia Stars	14–9	7–10
Baltimore Elite Giants	**13–9**	**12–8**
Newark Eagles	11–9	10–8
New York Cubans	3–11	3–9
New York Black Yankees	2–16	5–10

1946	1st Half	2nd Half
Newark Eagles	25–9	22–7
New York Cubans	13–13	15–8
Homestead Grays	18–15	9–13
Philadelphia Stars	17–12	10–17
Baltimore Elite Giants	**14–17**	**14–14**
New York Black Yankees	3–24	5–16

1947	1st Half Only
Newark Eagles	27–15
New York Cubans	20–12
Baltimore Elite Giants	**23–20**
Homestead Grays	19–20
Philadelphia Stars	13–16
New York Black Yankees	6–25

1948
No standings published for NAL East

1949	1st Half Only
Baltimore Elite Giants	**24–12**
New York Cubans	14–10
Philadelphia Stars	13–20
Indianapolis Clowns	14–23
Louisville Buckeyes	8–29

1950	1st Half	2nd Half
Indianapolis Clowns	29–17–1	18–21–1
Baltimore Elite Giants	**10–9–1**	**14–11**
New York Cubans	12–13	6–3
Philadelphia Stars	10–21–1	5–7
Cleveland Buckeyes	3–37	0–2

1951	1st Half	2nd Half
Indianapolis Clowns	29–12	24–14
Birmingham Black Barons	15–21	9–19
Philadelphia Stars	12–17	6–11
Balt-Nashville Elite Giants	**13–24**	**15–12**

Source: Dick Clark and Larry Lester, eds. *The Negro Leagues Book* (Cleveland, Ohio: Society for American Baseball Research) 1994, pp. 161–63. Used by permission.

NOTES

Prologue

1. Neil Lanctot. *Negro League Baseball: The Rise and Ruin of a Black Institution.* (Philadelphia: University of Pennsylvania Press) 2004, p. 175.

2. Frazier "Slow" Robinson with Paul Bauer. *Catching Dreams: My Life in the Negro Baseball Leagues.* (Syracuse, NY: Syracuse University Press) 1999, p. 140.

3. "Loop Head Orders Teams to Complete Friday Game." *The Afro-American.* September 25, 1948, p. 9.

4. "Elites Top Homestead in Playoff." *The Sun.* September 20, 1948, p. 13.

5. "Baltimore 'Stalled'; Grays Awarded Flag." *The Pittsburgh Courier.* October 2, 1948, p. 27.

6. Joe Black. *Ain't Nobody Better Than You: An Autobiography of Joe Black.* (Scottsdale, AZ: Ironwood Lithographers) 1983, p. 61.

7. Harold Gould interview. January 22, 2007.

8. Clinton "Butch" McCord interview. May 5, 2006.

9. "Leaders in Nashville City Life." *The Chicago Defender.* June 20, 1942, p. 9. James Hendrix. *I Remember Tom.* (Nashville, TN: Hamlet Printing Co.) 1983, p. 9.

10. McCord interview. May 5, 2006.

11. Roy Campanella. *It's Good to Be Alive.* (Boston: Little, Brown and Co.) 1959, p. 122.

12. Bill Glauber. "Elite Giants: The Pride of Baltimore Baseball History." *The Sun.* April 29, 1990, p. C12.

13. Brad Snyder. *Beyond the Shadow of the Senators: The Untold Story of the Homestead Grays and the Integration of Baseball.* (Chicago: Contemporary Books) 2003, p. 42.

14. Leslie A. Heaphy. *The Negro Leagues: 1869–1960.* (Jefferson, NC: McFarland & Co.) 2003, p. 119.

15. Eddie Gant. "I Cover the Eastern Front." *The Chicago Defender.* May 16, 1942, p. 21.

16. "Balto. School Board Remains Lily White." *The Afro-American.* March 19, 1938, p. 6.

17. "Blinded, Files Attack Count Against Police." *The Chicago Defender.* January 21, 1939, p. 10. W. A. C. Hughes, Jr., "Report of Legal Committee for 1938–39." NAACP Papers. Section II. Box C76. Folder 4. Manuscript Division. Library of Congress. Washington, DC.

18. Hughes. "Report of Legal Committee for 1938–39."

19. Ibid.

20. "Bus Driver Ousts Two Women on Highway." *The Afro-American.* September

13, 1941, p. 1. "News Release for the Afro." August 16, 1944. NAACP Papers. Section II. Box C77. Folder 2. Manuscript Division. Library of Congress. Washington, DC.

21. Robert J. Brugger. *Maryland: A Middle Temperament, 1634–1980*. (Baltimore: Johns Hopkins University Press) 1988, p. 560.

22. "News From Baltimore Branch NAACP" April, 1943. NAACP Papers. Section II. Box C76. Folder 4. Manuscript Division. Library of Congress. Washington, D.C. "City Library Above Federal Law—Trustees." The Afro-American, November 20, 1943, p. 10. "J.C. Still Boss at Md. Institute, Afro Artist Finds." *The Afro-American.* September 28, 1943, p. 15.

23. "Martin Says No Aircraft Jobs." *The Afro-American.* March 15, 1941, pp. 1, 5.

24. "President Orders an Even Break For Minorities in Defense Jobs." *The New York Times.* June 26, 1941, p. 12.

25. Cynthia Neverdon-Morton. "Black Housing Patterns in Baltimore City, 1885–1953." *The Maryland Historian.* Vol. 16. No. 1. Spring–Summer. 1985, p. 25.

26. Stanley Glenn interview. January 12, 2006.

27. "In The Negro Leagues: Baltimoreans Remember," p. 28. Section of a longer article from Charlotte Harvey's scrapbook with no other identifying information. Charlotte is the widow of Elite pitcher Bill Harvey.

28. Prentice Mills. "The People's Game As Remembered by Negro Leagues Fans." *Black Ball News.* Vol. 1. No. 6. 1993, p. 16.

29. Daniel Cattau. "Forgotten Heroes." *The Washington Post.* June 3, 1990, p. SM22.

30. Glenn interview.

Chapter 1 High Hopes

1. Neil Lanctot. *Negro League Baseball: The Rise and Ruin of a Black Institution.* (Philadelphia: University of Pennsylvania Press) 2004, p. 46.

2. Elizabeth Fee, Linda Shopes, and Linda Zeidman (eds.). *The Baltimore Book: New Views of Local History.* (Philadelphia: Temple University Press) 1991, pp. 204–205.

3. Roderick N. Ryon. "Old West Baltimore." *Maryland Historical Magazine.* Vol. 77. No. 1. March 1982, p. 55.

4. Ibid., p. 60.

5. Ibid., pp. 54, 60.

6. Cynthia Neverdon-Morton. "Black Housing Patterns in Baltimore City, 1885–1953." *The New York Times.* June 26, 1941, p. 33.

7. Tom Saunders interview, May 12 and October 25, 2006. Saunders is a community relations representative supervisor for the City of Baltimore and president of Renaissance Productions and Tours.

8. Ibid.

9. Interview with Charlotte Harvey, widow of Elite pitcher Bill Harvey and a graduate of Douglass High School in the class of 1930. September 19, 2007.

10. Suzanne Ellery Greene. *An Illustrated History of Baltimore* (Woodland Hill, CA: Windsor Publications, 1980), p. 193. "Victorine Adams: Civil Rights Leader, Humanitarian and Schoolteacher." *The Sun*. February 23, 2007.

11. J. Robert Smith. "Business Has Definite Future, Grocer Says." *The Afro-American*. May 21, 1938, p. 10.

12. J. Robert Smith. "Local Laundry Business Grosses $40,000 A Year." *The Afro-American*. March 26, 1938, p. 17.

13. Rosa Pryor-Truste and Tonya Taliaferro. *African American Entertainment in Baltimore*. (Charleston, SC: Arcadia Publications) 2003, p. 108.

14. Clarence Brown interview. September 2, 2006.

15. Ryon. "Old West Baltimore," p. 62.

16. Frederick Lonesome interview. October 10, 2006.

17. Harold A. McDougall. *Black Baltimore: A New Theory of Community*. (Philadelphia: Temple University Press) 1993, pp. 41–51.

18. Ryon. "Old West Baltimore," p. 57.

19. Greene. *An Illustrated History of Baltimore*, p. 200.

20. "Business League Ends Biggest Meet." *The Chicago Defender*. September 4, 1943, p. 20.

21. "Address of Theodore R. McKeldin, 43rd Annual Convention of the National Negro Business League and Housewives League, Bethel AME Church, Druid Hill Avenue and Lanvale Street. August 25, 1943." Papers of Theodore Roosevelt McKeldin. Hornbake Library. University of Maryland Library. College Park, Maryland. Series I. Box I. Speeches 1930–1945.

22. Evelena D. Jackson. "Hayes Pleases Huge Audience at Sharp Street." *The Afro-American*. November 6, 1943, p. 8.

23. Ryon. "Old West Baltimore," p. 66.

24. 1947 Elite Giant Program.

25. Saunders interview.

26. Greene. *An Illustrated History of Baltimore*, p. 193.

27. *http://citypaper.com/news/story.asp?id=9603*. Accessed June 12, 2006.

28. Brown interview.

29. Lonesome interview.

30. Greene. *An Illustrated History of Baltimore*, p. 192.

31. Lonesome interview.

32. "Richard Powell Obituary." *Negro League Baseball Players Association*. *http://nlbpa.com/3feb2004.html*. Accessed January 4, 2006.

33. Robert V. Leffler, Jr. *"Boom and Bust: The Elite Giants and Black Baseball in Baltimore, 1936–1951." Maryland Historical Magazine*. Vol. 87. No. 2. Summer 1992, p. 171.

34. "Frontiers Club Meets Aug. 5–8." *The Chicago Defender*. July 31, 1948, p. 3.

35. Vernon Green Estate Papers, Thurgood Marshall Law Library, Baltimore.

36. "Vernon Green Succumbs to Heart Attack in Baltimore." *The Afro-American*. June 4, 1949. Section 2, p. 4.

37. James A. Riley. *The Biographical Encyclopedia of the Negro Baseball Leagues*. (New York: Carroll & Graf Publishers, Inc.) 1994, p. 639.

38. Barbara Powell Golden interview. April 27, 2006.

39. "Wilson May Transfer Elite Giants From Washington to Balto." *The Afro-American*. February 5, 1938, p. 18.

40. "Richard Powell Obituary."

41. Mark Kram. "It Seemed Like It Happened in Another Century." *Baltimore News American*. August 9, 1981, p. 2E.

42. "Negro League Ball in Good Shape." *The Philadelphia Tribune*. April 3, 1930, p. 11.

43. Arthur Mann. *The Jackie Robinson Story*. (New York: Grosset & Dunlap) 1950, p.18.

44. That Smith is black can be seen in a photograph of team owners and NNL officials in which he appears. *The Afro-American*. January 11, 1941, p. 19.

45. "May Transfer Elite Giants From Washington to Balto.," p. 18.

46. Red Smith. "Remembrances of Eddie Gottlieb." *The New York Times*. January 13, 1980.

47. Steven A. Riess (ed.). *Sports and the American Jew*. (Syracuse, NY: Syracuse University Press) 1998, p. 27.

48. "Elites to Use Oriole Park." *The Afro-American*. April 10, 1937, p. 20.

49. Ibid. The astute Negro league fan will know that Willie Wells of the Newark Eagles was on none of the teams during the regular season. It was not uncommon for star players to be signed by another team for a championship series.

50. Leon Hardwick. "Chicago Gets An Even Split With Grays." *The Afro-American*. October 2, 1937, p. 19.

51. Leffler. "Boom and Bust," p. 171.

52. Edward C. Lastner. "I Remember ... Bugle Field and the Label Men." *The Sun Magazine*. March 29, 1953, p. 2.

53. Lonesome interview.

54. Ibid.

55. 1947 Second Half Baltimore Elite Giants Program.

56. Lonesome interview.

57. Clinton "Butch" McCord interview. May 5, 2006.

58. Interview with Frank Lynch, December 5, 2006, at a meeting of the Maryland Old-Timers Baseball Association, Baltimore.

59. George Henderson interview. January 18, 2007.

60. Charlotte Harvey interview.

61. Lonesome interview.

62. Irving Morris interview. October 10, 2006.

63. Interview with Thomas Cripps, University Distinguished Professor (retired) at Morgan State University in Baltimore. May 19, 2007.

64. Ibid.

65. Lynch interview.

66. Bill Glauber. "Elite Giants: The Pride of Baltimore Baseball History." *The Sun.* April 29, 1990, p. C1.

67. John Holway. *Voices From the Great Black Baseball Leagues.* (New York: Dodd, Mead & Co.) 1975, p. 332.

68. Clinton "Butch" McCord interview. October 18, 2006. I didn't find a statement of the exact distances at Bugle Field but Paul Bonomo, who played sandlot baseball at Bugle, remembers "it was 420 feet in right and 389 feet in left" (interview with Paul Bonomo, December 5, 2006, at a meeting of the Maryland Old-Timers Baseball Association. Baltimore). The number 420 appears on the fence in centerfield in the background of some photographs taken at Bugle Field.

69. Fee, Shopes, and Zeidman. *The Baltimore Book*, p. 203.

70. Riley. *Biographical Encyclopedia,* pp. 503–504.

71. Buck Leonard with James A. Riley. *Buck Leonard: The Black Lou Gehrig.* (New York: Carroll & Graf) 1995, p. 111.

72. Roy Campanella. *It's Good to Be Alive* (New York: Little, Brown and Co.) 1959. pp. 58–59.

73. Ibid., p. 67.

74. Ibid., p. 165.

75. Ibid., p. 66.

76. Ibid., pp. 55–56.

77. James "Red" Moore interview. January 19, 2006.

78. Michael Benson. *Ballparks in North America: A Comprehensive Historical Reference to Baseball Grounds, Yards, and Stadiums 1845 to Present.* (Jefferson, NC: McFarland & Co.) 1989, p. 25.

79. Ibid., p. 830.

80. Art Carter Papers, Box 170-19. Folder 9. Manuscript Division, Moorland-Spingarn Research Center, Howard University.

81. Riley. *Biographical Encyclopedia.* pp. 400–401.

82. Art Carter Papers, Box 170-19. Folder 10.

83. Article written on Hughes by John Holway based on a 1972 interview. Art Carter Papers, Box 170-17. Folder 5.

84. Ibid.

85. Glauber. "Elite Giants: The pride," p. C1.

86. Riley. *Biographical Encyclopedia,* p. 808

87. "Tom Wilson Takes Club to Baltimore." *The Chicago Defender.* April 2, 1938, p. 8.

88. Riley. *Biographical Encyclopedia,* p. 463.

89. James H. Bready. "The Remembrances of Two Old-Timers." *The Sun.* November 5, 1996, p. 9A.

90. Leonard and Riley. *Buck Leonard,* pp. 110–111.

91. Riley. *Biographical Encyclopedia,* pp. 881–882.

92. Bill Glauber. "Elite Giants: Great Players, Even Greater Personalities." *The Sun.* April 30, 1990, p. C6.

93. Riley. *Biographical Encyclopedia,* pp. 881–882.

94. Leonard and Riley. *Buck Leonard,* p. 110.

95. Riley. *Biographical Encyclopedia,* p. 882.

96. Ibid., p. 394.

97. Ibid., p. 636.

98. Ibid., p. 140.

99. Campanella. *It's Good to Be Alive,* p. 66.

100. Ibid., p. 299.

101. Ibid., p. 60.

102. "Chicago Wins 3 to 0; Memphis Downs Baltimore." *The Chicago Defender.* April 16, 1938, p. 22.

103. Telephone interview with James "Red" Moore. October 2, 2006. Moore was with the Elites in 1939 and 1940 and could not vouch for sure that the same uniform was used in 1938. I think the chances are good that it was. Money was always tight and new uniforms for an entire team would have been a large expense. The fact that no city name appeared on the uniform would have allowed the uniform to be used in any of the cities the Elites called home.

104. "Chicago Wins 3 to 0," p. 22.

105. "NNL Campaign Begins on Saturday." *The Afro-American.* May 14, 1938, p. 23.

106. "Elites Trounce Philly Stars in Opener 17–8." *The Afro-American.* May 21, 1938, p. 23.

107. Dick Clark and Larry Lester (eds.). *The Negro Leagues Book.* (Cleveland: Society for American Baseball Research) 1994, p. 161.

108. "D.C. Senators Down Elites." *The Afro-American.* July 23, 1938, p. 22.

109. "Stars Lose 2 to Balto.; Top Yanks." *The Afro-American.* September 10, 1938, p. 23.

110. Gus Greenlee and Cum Posey. "NNL Turns in Report." *The Afro-American.* September 10, 1938, p. 23.

Chapter 2 Pennants and Jumpers

1. "Elite Giants on 9-Day Road Trip." *The Afro-American.* April 15, 1939, p. 21.

2. James A. Riley. *The Biographical Encyclopedia of the Negro Baseball Leagues* (New York: Carroll & Graf Publishers, Inc.) 1994, p. 699.

3. Bill Glauber. "Elite Giants: The Pride of Baltimore Baseball History." *The Sun.* April 29, 1990, p. C12.

4. Jules Tygiel. *Baseball's Great Experiment: Jackie Robinson and His Legacy.* (Cary, NC: Oxford University Press) 1983, p. 18.

5. Rudy Marzano. *The Brooklyn Dodgers in the 1940s: How Robinson, MacPhail, and Rickey Changed Baseball.* (Jefferson, NC: McFarland & Co.) 2005, p. 181.

6. *The Afro-American.* May 27, 1939, p. 11.

7. "Homestead Grays Hand Double Beating to Baltimore." *The Chicago Defender.* May 20, 1939, p. 9.

8. Peter Jackson. "Elites, Yankees Win in Yankee Stadium." *The Afro-American.* June 10, 1939, p. 21.

9. Michael O'Keefe. "Yankees Should Honor the Past." *New York Daily News.* September 8, 2003, p. 67.

10. David Marasco. "The Jacob Ruppert Memorial Cup." *The Diamond Angle.* http://www.thediamondangle.com/marasco/negleg/ruppert.html. Accessed November 23, 2004.

11. "Black Yankees Bow, 4–0." *The New York Times.* July 3, 1939, p. 13.

12. "Five Atlanta Players Signed by Baltimore." *The Chicago Defender.* July 22, 1939, p. 8.

13. Ibid., p. 139.

14. John Holway. *Voices from the Great Black Baseball Leagues* (New York: Dodd, Mead & Co.) 1975, p. 328.

15. Ibid., p. 332.

16. James "Red" Moore interview. January 19, 2006.

17. *The Afro-American.* August 12, 1939, p. 17.

18. Dick Clark and Larry Lester (eds.) *The Negro Leagues Book.* (Cleveland: Society for American Baseball Research) 1994, p. 161. A playoff that matches the first and fourth place finishers and the second and third place finishers is commonly referred to as the Shaughnessy Playoff System in honor of International League President Frank Shaughnessey who invented it in 1932. (Northern League Championship Formats *http://www.snake.net/nl/stats/playoffs/championship-formats.html.* Accessed March 1, 2006.)

19. Ralph Boyd. "Elites Whip Eagles." *The Afro-American.* September 16, 1939, p. 23.

20. Art Carter. "Elites, Grays Tied in National League Series." *The Afro-American.* September 23, 1939, p. 19.

21. "Homestead Grays, Elites Divide Pair." *The Chicago Defender.* September 23, 1939, p. 8.

22. "Elite Giants Win National League Championship." *The Afro-American.* September 30, 1939, p. 21.

23. John Holway. *The Complete Book of Baseball's Negro Leagues: The Other Half of Baseball History.* (Fern Park, FL: Hastings House) 2004, p. 367.

24. Riley. *Biographical Encyclopedia*, p. 399.

25. "Elites Win National League Championship," p. 21.

26. Art Carter Papers, Box 170-16. Folder 1. Manuscript Division, Moorland-Spingarn Research Center, Howard University.

27. Stationery and envelope found in ibid., Folder 12.

28. Buck Leonard and James A. Riley. *Buck Leonard: The Black Lou Gehrig.* (New York: Carroll & Graf Publishers) 1995, p. 112.

29. "Tom Wilson New National League Head." *The Chicago Defender.* March 3, 1939, p. 8.

30. Riley. *The Biographical Encyclopedia,* p. 629.

31. "Posey's Points." *The Pittsburgh Courier.* October 21, 1939, p. 17.

32. Ibid., pp. 79–80.

33. Telegram from Tom Wilson to Effa Manley. Effa Manley, Newark Eagles Papers. Charles F. Cummings New Jersey Information Room. Newark Public Library. Newark, NJ.

34. Dan Burley. "Posey Walks Out As Effa Manley Loses; Blast on Standpats." *The Pittsburgh Courier.* February 17, 1940.

35. "Row May Split National League." *The Chicago Defender.* February 24, 1940, p. 24.

36. Neil Lanctot. *Negro League Baseball: The Rise and Ruin of a Black Institution.* (Philadelphia: University of Pennsylvania Press) 2004, p. 89.

37. "Owners Fail to Elect." *The Chicago Defender.* March 2, 1940, p. 24.

38. Randy Dixon. "The Sports Bugle." *The Pittsburgh Courier.* February 17, 1940.

39. Lanctot. *Negro League Baseball,* p. 310.

40. August 1, 1941, letter from Effa Manley to Cum Posey. Effa Manley, Newark Eagles Papers. Charles F. Cummings New Jersey Information Room. Newark Public Library. Newark, NJ.

41. Ibid.

42. Butts Brown. "In The Groove." *The Newark Herald.* September 16, 1944, p. 12.

43. Lanctot. *Negro League Baseball,* p. 151.

44. "Bolden Says Stars Should be Playing." *The New York Amsterdam News.* September 16, 1944. No page number. Hall of Fame, Cooperstown, NY. Ed Bolden file.

45. Lanctot. *Negro League Baseball,* p. 150.

46. Lucius C. Harper. "Dustin' off the News." *The Chicago Defender.* August 19, 1939, p. 1.

47. Larry Lester. *Black Baseball's National Showcase: The East-West All-Star Game 1933–1953*. (Lincoln: University of Nebraska Press) 2001, pp. 21–22.

48. "Minister Elected Head of Negro National League." *The Chicago Defender*. January 11, 1947, p. 1.

49. "Tom Wilson Threatens To Use Big Club." *The Chicago Defender*. May 24, 1941, p. 23.

50. "Campanella, Hughes Cited for Fine, Suspension." *The Afro-American*. August 15, 1942, p. 26.

51. "'Dream Game' Box Score." *The Afro-American*. August 22, 1942, p. 16.

52. Roy Campanella. *It's Good to Be Alive*. (Boston: Little, Brown and Co.) 1959, p. 58. Milton J. Shapiro. *The Roy Campanella Story*. (New York: Julian Messner, Inc.) 1958, p. 59.

53. "Owners Bar League Ball Clubs From Playing Clowns." *The Chicago Defender*. January 3, 1942, p. 24.

54. Sam Lacy. "Two Homestead Gray Stars in Bad With Officials, One Suspended." *The Afro-American*. May 27, 1944, p. 18.

55. Fay Young. "Through The Years." *The Chicago Defender*. July 14, 1945, p. 7.

56. "Hint Grays May Trade Josh Gibson to Elites." *The Afro-American*. February 3, 1940, p. 20.

57. Riley. *Biographical Encyclopedia*, pp. 140, 323, 881.

58. Mark Kram. "It Seemed Like It Happened in Another Century." *Baltimore News American*. August 9, 1981, p. 3E.

59. Art Carter. "Elites Play Stars Twin Bill Sunday." *The Afro-American*. May 11, 1940, p. 23.

60. "Elites Sweep Opening Series." *The Afro-American*. May 18, 1940, p. 20.

61. Ibid.

62. Sam Lacy. "Elites Gain Edge in Series." *Afro-American*. May 25, 1940, p. 19.

63. Art Carter. "5,000 See Elites and Yanks Split." *The Afro-American*. June 29, 1940, p. 22.

64. "Elites Lose Lead in N.L.L. Race." *The Afro-American*. July 6, 1940, p. 21.

65. "Elites Wallop Grays." *The Afro-American*. July 20, 1940, p. 19.

66. Art Carter. "Ray Brown Blanks Foes for 12th Win." *The Afro-American*. August 3, 1940, p. 19.

67. Sam Lacy. "Grays Defeat Elites Twice to Clinch League Crown." *The Afro-American*. September 7, 1940, p. 19.

68. "Elites Win Trophy." *The New York Times*. September 9, 1940, p. 21.

69. "Elites Swap 7 Men in 11 Player Deal with Yanks." *The Afro-American*. January 4, 1941, p. 21.

70. "Elites and Yanks Swap Six Players." *The Afro-American*. January 11, 1941, p. 19.

71. "Leagues Lift Player Ban." *The Afro-American*. March 1, 1941, p. 19.

72. Ibid.

73. "Wilson Re-Casts Team." *The Afro-American*. April 12, 1941, p. 21.

74. Moore interview, January 19, 2006.

75. "Elites Win 6–5, After 9–6 Defeat." *The Afro-American*. May 10, 1941, p. 19.

76. Ibid.

77. "Elite Giants Bow to Grays, 13–11." *The Washington Post*. May 11, 1941, p. S2.

78. Art Carter. "6,000 Watch Grays, Elites Break Even." *The Afro-American*. May 17, 1941, p. 19.

79. Peter L. Jackson. "Cubans Beat Elites." *The Afro-American*. June 7, 1941, p. 19.

80. "Campanella's .579 Tops NNL Batters." *The Afro-American*. June 14, 1941, p. 21.

81. "Elites Shade Memphis Red Sox." *The Afro-American*. July 19, 1941, p. 19.

82. "Monarchs Beaten by Elites, 4–2." *The Afro-American*. July 26, 1941, p. 21.

83. "Campanella Voted 'Most Valuable.'" *The Afro-American*. August 21, 1941, p. 19.

84. Russ J. Cowans. "Elites and Grays Split Double Bill." *The Afro-American*. August 9, 1941, p. 21.

85. Dick Powell. "Elites in Split with Monarchs." *The Afro-American*. August 23, 1941, p. 23.

86. Dick Powell. "Elites Nip St. Louis as Lefty Gaines Fans 19." *The Afro-American*. August 23, 1941, p. 22.

87. "Standings." *The Chicago Defender*. August 30, 1941, p. 23.

88. "Elites Down Grays in Twin Bill." *The Washington Post*. August 25, 1941, p. 17.

89. "Results." *The Chicago Defender*. September 6, 1941, p. 24.

90. Clark and Lester, *The Negro Leagues Book*, p. 161.

91. Brad Snyder. *Beyond the Shadow of the Senators: The Untold Story of the Homestead Grays and the Integration of Baseball*. (Chicago: Contemporary Books) 2003, p. 52.

92. Art Carter. "Phils May Bid for Catcher." *The Afro-American*. July 25, 1942, p. 22.

93. "Bus Driver Ousts Two Women on Highway." *The Afro-American*. September 13, 1941, p. 1.

94. Roderick N. Ryon. "Old West Baltimore." *Maryland Historical Magazine*. Vol. 77. No. 1. March 1982, p. 64.

95. Elizabeth Fee, Linda Shopes, and Linda Zeidman (eds.). *The Baltimore Book: New Views of Local History*. (Philadelphia: Temple University Press) 1991, p. 192.

Chapter 3 War on the Home Front

1. *http://www.oah.org/pubs/magazine/sport/percoco.html*. Accessed March 10, 2006.

2. Robert J. Brugger. *Maryland: A Middle Temperament, 1634–1980*. (Baltimore: Johns Hopkins University Press) 1988, p. 529.

3. Ibid., p. 532.

4. "Elites Play Philly Stars in Baltimore." *The Chicago Defender*. May 9, 1942, p. 19.

5. Art Carter. "Record Crowd in Offing for Games." *The Afro-American*. May 5, 1942, p. 24.

6. "Rally in 10th Wins First Game," "Elites Spoil Stars' Opening." *The Afro-American*. May 16, 1942, p. 23.

7. Robert V. Leffler, Jr. "The History of Black Baseball in Baltimore from 1913 to 1951." Master's thesis, Morgan State University, 1974, p. 87.

8. "Grays, Elites Split Twin-Bill." *The Afro-American*. May 23, 1942, p. 21.

9. "Baltimore Wins First Half in National League." *The Chicago Defender*. July 11, 1942, p. 21.

10. Ibid.

11. *http://www.baseballlibrary.com/baseballlibrary/ballplayers/B/Byrd_Bill.stm*. Accessed June 23, 2006.

12. Buck Leonard with James A. Riley. *Buck Leonard: The Black Lou Gehrig* (New York: Carroll & Graf) 1995, p. 101.

13. Art Carter. "Snow Plans Protest of Fine to League." *The Afro-American*. July 25, 1942, p. 22.

14. "Elites Drop 3 Straight as Grays Take Twin Bill." *The Afro-American*. August 1, 1942, p. 23.

15. *http://www.nlbpa.com/day__leon.html*. For the record, Satchel Paige tied Day's performance by striking out 18 Philadelphia Stars on September 9, 1934, to give the Crawfords a 3–1 victory. (Lawrence D. Hogan. *Shades of Glory*. [Washington, DC: National Geographic] 2006, p. 268.)

16. "Catcher Jumps to Mexico." *The Afro-American*. August 29, 1942, p. 25.

17. George Lyle, Jr. "Elites Lose Two Out of Five Tilts to Stars." *The Afro-American*. September 12, 1942, p. 23.

18. Ibid.

19. "30,000 May See D.C. Tilt." *The Afro-American*. September 8, 1942, p. 19.

20. Charles Osgood. *Defending Baltimore Against the Enemy*. (New York: Hyperion Press) 2004, p. 46.

21. Ibid.

22. Peter Morris. *A Game of Inches: The Game Behind the Scenes*. (Chicago: Ivan R. Dee Publisher) 2006, p. 333.

23. William B. Mead and Paul Dickson. *Baseball: The Presidents' Game*. (Washington, DC.: Farragut Publishing Co.) 1993, p. 199.

24. Ibid., p. 76.

25. "Elites Win, Lose With Newark," *The Chicago Defender*. May 23, 1936, p. 13.

26. "Elites Win Opener." *The Afro-American*. May 8, 1937, p. 21.

27. "Elites Sweep Opening Day Games." *The Afro-American*. May 18, 1940, p. 20. "Rally in 10th Wins First Game." *The Afro-American*. May 16, 1942, p. 23. "Grays Meet

Baltimore In Two Double Headers." *The Chicago Defender*. May 29, 1943, p. 11. "Elites Trounce Stars 15–5, 9–0." *The Afro-American*. May 13, 1944, p. 14.

28. From an ad in the Baltimore Elite Giant program for the second half of 1947.

29. "Many Officials Pay Tribute At Marse Callaway Funeral." *The Sun*. May 24, 1959. "Callaway Dead." *The Sun*. May 20, 1959.

30. "Willie Adams." *Baltimore Magazine*. January 1979, pp. 58–59.

31. Ted Waters. "Numbers Found Lucrative Industry." *The Afro-American*. February 8, 1947, p. 7.

32. "Willie Adams," pp. 58, 59. "Willie Adams Acquitted." *The News American*. June 20, 1984.

33. Clarence Brown interview. September 2, 2006.

34. "Willie Adams," pp. 58, 59. "Willie Adams Acquitted."

35. "Baltimore's Legendary Business Leader Raps on Black Survival." *The Afro-American*. May 31, 1977.

36. Early Byrd. "Little Willie." *The Afro-American*. April 17, 2004, p. A11.

37. "Inaugural Address of Theodore Roosevelt McKeldin As Mayor of Baltimore, May 18, 1943. Papers of Theodore Roosevelt McKeldin. Hornbake Library. University of Maryland Library. College Park, Maryland. Series I. Box I. Speeches 1930–1945.

38. Ronald A. Rooks interview. October 3, 2006. Mr. Rooks, an appraiser of art and antiques, is a Baltimore native and attended several games at Westport Stadium.

39. Letter from Theodore R. McKeldin to Randall L. Tyrus. June 26, 1943. McKeldin Files. Box 260, File T-20. Baltimore City Archives.

40. "Maryland U. to Seek Ruling on Racial Bars." *The Washington Post*. December 14, 1950, p. B1.

41. "Statement of Mayor Theodore R. McKeldin in Appointment of an Advisory Committee on City Housing. May 5th, 1945." McKeldin Files. Box 259. Folder T-10. Baltimore City Archives.

42. Victor E. Schminke letter to McKeldin. May 7, 1945. In ibid.

43. Addison V. Pinkney letter to McKeldin. July 26, 1945. McKeldin File. Box 253. File G1-48-(2).

44. "Strike of 100 Causes 30,000 to Lose a Day." *The Afro-American*. November 6, 1943, p. 7.

45. "Coast Guard Unit Turns Down 3 More Volunteers." *The Afro-American*. November 20, 1943, p. 10.

46. "W. Elec. Tells WLB Separate Facilities Will Stem War Work." *The Afro-American*. November 20, 1943, p. 10.

47. "News From Baltimore Branch NAACP." April, 1943. NAACP Papers. Section II. Box C76. Folder 4. Manuscript Division. Library of Congress. Washington, DC.

48. Letter of Enoch Pratt Formally Transferring the Management of the Library to the Board of Trustees. October 1, 1884.

49. Dick Powell. "Baltimore Gets Ready." *The Chicago Defender.* April 24, 1943, p. 21.

50. Dick Clark and Larry Lester (eds.). *The Negro Leagues Book* (Cleveland: Society for American Baseball Research) 1994, p.132.

51. Art Carter. "NNL Votes to 'Carry On.'" *The Afro-American.* April 10, 1943, p. 19.

52. "May Resign." *The Afro-American.* January 23, 1943, p. 19, photo caption.

53. James A. Riley. *The Biographical Encyclopedia of the Negro Baseball Leagues.* (New York: Carroll & Graf), p. 502.

54. Dick Powell. "Four Baltimore Players Will Keep Defense Jobs." *The Chicago Defender.* March 27, 1943, p. 21.

55. "Mayor to Throw Out Ball as Elites Play Grays Sunday." *The Afro-American.* May 29, 1943, p. 14.

56. "Gibson Big Gun as Elites Bow to Grays." *The Afro-American.* May 22, 1943. "Elites Beat Grays Twice." *The Afro-American.* May 29, 1943, p. 23.

57. Art Carter. "Elites Beat Grays Twice." *The Afro-American.* June 5, 1943, p. 22.

58. Theodore McKeldin's Appointment Book, 1943. Papers of Theodore Roosevelt McKeldin. Hornbake Library. University of Maryland Library. College Park, Maryland. Series II. Box I. Office Files.

59. Carter. "Elites Beat Grays Twice."

60. "Grays Sweep 4-Game Elite Series." *The Afro-American.* August 28, 1943, p. 23.

61. Riley. *The Biographical Encyclopedia,* pp. 401, 299, 86, 367.

62. Arch Ward. "In The Wake of the News." *The Chicago Defender.* September 9, 1952, p. B1.

63. Telephone conversation with Jarrett Carter, Alumni Office, Morgan State University. December 2, 2006.

64. John Holway. *Voices from the Great Black Baseball Leagues* (New York: Dodd, Mead & Co.) 1975, p. 158.

65. Ibid., p. 333.

66. Joe Black. *Ain't Nobody Better Than You: An Autobiography of Joe Black* (Scottsdale, AZ: Ironwood Lithographers) 1983, p. 65.

67. Bill Glauber. "Elite Giants: Great Players, Even Greater Personalities." *The Sun.* April 30, 1990, p. C6.

68. "Elites Take Twin Bill from All-Stars for 3rd Straight." *The Afro-American.* September 27, 1943, p. 23.

69. "Elites Lose to All-Stars. *The Afro-American.* October 16, 1943.

70. John Holway. *The Complete Book of Baseball's Negro Leagues: The Other Half of Baseball History.* (Fern Park, FL: Hastings House) 2004, p. 413.

71. "Hall Refused for Robeson." *The Afro-American.* March 18, 1944, p. 1.

72. "City Library Above Federal Law—Trustees." *The Afro-American.* November 20, 1943, p. 10.

73. "Judge Dismisses Library Lawsuit." *The Sun.* March 8, 1944.

74. "The Monumental City." *The Afro-American.* April 1, 1944, p. 15.

75. "Return of Campanella, Butts Lifts Elite Hopes." *The Afro-American.* April 22, 1944, p. 14.

76. Roy Campanella. *It's Good to Be Alive* (Boston: Little, Brown and Co.) 1959, p. 61.

77. "Return of Campanella," p. 14.

78. "Elites Trounce Stars in NNL Opening, 15–5, 9–0." *The Afro-American.* May 13, 1944, p. 14.

79. Theodore McKeldin's Appointment Books, 1943–1947. Papers of Theodore Roosevelt McKeldin. Hornbake Library. University of Maryland Library. College Park, Maryland. Series II. Box 1. Office Files.

80. "Elites Trounce Stars 15–5, 9–0." *The Afro-American.* May 13, 1944, p. 14.

81. "Grays, Stars to Play Night Tilt Thursday." *The Washington Post.* May 22, 1944, p. 12.

82. Sam Lacy. "Grays Beat Eagles; Lead Eagles by Two Games." *The Afro-American.* June 3, 1944, p. 18.

83. "Balto. Takes 3 of 4 from Newark." *The Afro-American.* June 10, 1944, p. 18. "Baltimore and Cubans Divide." *The Chicago Defender.* July 1, 1944, p. 9. "Elites Take Two of Three from League Leaders." *The Afro-American.* July 1, 1944, p. 18.

84. "Statement of Mayor Theodore H. McKeldin." August 30, 1944. McKeldin File. RG9 S22. Box 259. File T-16.

85. "Elites Beat Eagles," "Elites 11, Eagles 6." *The Chicago Defender.* July 22, 1944, p. 7.

86. "Elites Humble Yanks in Sweeping 3-Game Series." *The Afro-American.* July 29, 1944, p. 18.

87. "Diamond Dust." *The Afro-American.* September 9, 1944, p. 18.

88. "Phil. Stars Down Elites; Newark Trounces Cubans." *The Chicago Defender.* August 5, 1944, p. 7.

89. "Travel—Free State Style." *The Afro-American.* January 20, 1945, p. 4.

90. "Pratt Library Held Public Institution." *The Sun.* April 18, 1945. "Library to Accept Court Ruling." *The Sun.* April 18, 1945. "Pratt to Ask For Supreme Court Ruling." *The Sun.* April 24, 1945. "Library Case Declined by High Tribunal." *The Sun.* October 9, 1945.

91. "Officials to Confer on Bad Housing." *The Afro-American.* September 1, 1945, p. 5.

92. "Travel—Free State Style."

93. "Opinion: The Governor's Commission." *The Afro-American.* October 20, 1945, p. 4.

94. "Elites at Atlanta for Conditioning." *The Afro-American.* March 31, 1945, p. 18.

95. "Baltimore and Philadelphia Split." *The Chicago Defender.* May 12, 1945, p. 8.

96. "Elites Split with Philly Stars in NNL Inaugural." *The Afro-American.* May 12, 1945, p. 27.

97. "Grays Whitewash Elites in Detroit Bill, 1–0; 5–0." *The Afro-American.* June 9, 1945, p. 18.

98. Fay Young. "Through the Years." *The Chicago Defender.* July 14, 1945, p. 7.

99. Quoted in Neil Lanctot. *Negro League Baseball: The Rise and Ruin of a Black Institution* (Philadelphia: University of Pennsylvania Press) 2004, p. 171.

100. "Tom Glover, Elite Hurler in Mexico." *The Afro-American.* August 11, 1945, p. 18.

101. Sam Lacy. "Baltimore Misses Chance to Grab Lead in Philly Split." *The Afro-American.* September 1, 1945, p. 18.

102. "Grays Twice Down Elites to Win 6th NNL Pennant." *The Afro-American.* September 15, 1945, p. 22.

103. "Cubans Top Black Barons." *The New York Times.* October 1, 1945, p. 25.

104. "Orioles Humbled, 3–1, 4–3 by Balto. Elites." *The Afro-American.* October 13, 1945, p. 22.

105. Interview with Fred Trout. December 5, 2006 at meeting of the Maryland Old-Timers Baseball Association. Baltimore, Maryland.

106. Monte Irvin interview. January 12, 2007.

Chapter 4 Bending the Color Bar

1. Dick Clark and Larry Lester (eds.) *The Negro Leagues Book.* (Cleveland: Society for American Baseball Research) 1994, pp. 139–140.

2. "Idle Workers Pose Problems." *The Afro-American.* August 25, 1945, pp. 1, 24.

3. Snow Eyes Ills of Elites." *The Afro-American.* March 30, 1946, p. 18.

4. Sam Lacy. "Balto. Catcher Rumored En Route to Ill. Club." *The Afro-American.* April 6, 1946, p. 18.

5. "Dodgers Sign More Negroes." *The Chicago Defender.* April 13, 1946, p. 11.

6. Sam Lacy. "Rickey Signs Campanella for Nashua." *The Afro-American.* April 13, 1946, p. 18.

7. Roy Campanella. *It's Good to Be Alive.* (Boston: Little, Brown and Co.) 1959, pp. 97–98.

8. Harvey Frommer. *Rickey and Robinson* (New York: Macmillan Co.), 1982, pp. 110–111.

9. Larry Moffi and Jonathan Kronstadt. *Crossing the Line: Black Major Leaguers, 1947–1959.* (Iowa City: University of Iowa Press.) 1994, p. 28.

10. The Brooklyn Baseball Club. "The Case Against Jimmy Powers." Branch

Rickey Papers. Box 34. Folder 6. Manuscript Division. Library of Congress. Washington, DC.

11. Campanella. *It's Good to Be Alive*, pp. 122–123.

12. From Newark Eagles Team File, National Baseball Hall of Fame, Cooperstown, NY.

13. Letter signed by Cum Posey and edited by Effa Manley, dated November 1, 1945. Newark Eagles Team File, National Baseball Hall of Fame, Cooperstown, NY.

14. "Chandler Sees Martin, Wilson." *The Chicago Defender*. January 26, 1946.

15. Paul Dickson. *The Dickson Baseball Dictionary*. (New York: Facts on File) 1989, p. 322.

16. Gai Ingham Berlage. *Women in Baseball: The Forgotten History*. (Westport, CT: Praeger) 1994, p. 124.

17. Donn Rogosin. *Invisible Men: Life in Baseball's Negro Leagues*. (New York: Atheneum) 1983, p. 216.

18. Ibid., p. 178.

19. Letter from Branch Rickey to Henry J. Walsh. November 29, 1947. Branch Rickey Papers. Box 33, Folder 15. Manuscript Division. Library of Congress. Washington, DC.

20. Dick Powell. "Baltimore Looks Good Even Without Campanella, Wright." *The Chicago Defender*. April 20, 1946, p. 10.

21. "Snow Works Hard on Elite Defense." *The Afro-American*. April 20, 1946, p. 14.

22. James A. Riley. *The Biographical Encyclopedia of the Negro Baseball Leagues*. (New York: Carroll & Graf Publishers, Inc.) 1944, p. 330.

23. Arthur Mann. *The Jackie Robinson Story*. (New York: Grosset & Dunlap) 1950, pp. 24–25.

24. Sam Lacy. "Player Indifferent About Entering Major Leagues." *The Afro-American*. August 5, 1939, p. 22.

25. "Jackie's Errors Fatal to Montreal in Baltimore." *The Afro-American*. May 4, 1946, p. 15.

26. "Exciting Debut of Negro." *The Christian Science Monitor*. April 19, 1946, p. 15.

27. Arthur Mann. *Branch Rickey: American in Action*. (New York: Houghton-Mifflin) 1957, pp. 255–256.

28. Frommer. *Rickey and Robinson*, pp. 120–121.

29. Jackie Robinson, with Alfred Duckett. *I Never Had It Made*. (New York: G. P. Putnam's Sons) 1972, p. 59.

30. "Biased Baltimore Fans Slur Jackie Robinson During Recent Series." *The Afro-American*. May 4, 1946, p. 26.

31. Robinson. *I Never Had It Made*, p. 59.

32. Interview with Frank Lynch, December 5, 2006, at a meeting of The Maryland Old-Timers Baseball Association. Baltimore, Maryland.

33. Murray Polner. *Branch Rickey: A Biography*. (New York: Atheneum) 1982, p. 182.

34. John Steadman. "Baltimore Was Major-League Test: Robinson 50 Years Ago." *The Sun*. April 28, 1966, p. 2F.

35. "Elites Open 4 Game Series with Pace-Setting Birds." *The Afro-American*. May 18, 1946, p. 30.

36. Theodore McKeldin's Appointment Book, 1946. Papers of Theodore Roosevelt McKeldin. Hornbake Library. University of Maryland Library. College Park, Maryland. Series II. Box I. Office Files.

37. "Around and About With the NNL Baseball Teams." *The Afro-American*. May 18, 1946, p. 14.

38. "Grays to Meet Elites Tomorrow." *The Washington Post*. May 29, 1946, p. 13.

39. For an extensive discussion of his career and life, see Bob Luke. *Willie Wells: "El Diablo" of the Negro Leagues*. (Austin: University of Texas Press) 2007.

40. James A. Riley. *The Biographical Encyclopedia of the Negro Baseball Leagues*. (New York: Carroll & Graf) 1994, p. 401.

41. "Meet Junior Gilliam! International League's 1952 MVP." *Our Sport*. (Jackie Robinson ed.) June, 1953, p. 57.

42. Jackie Robinson and Charles Dexter. *Baseball Has Done It*. (Philadelphia: Lippincott) 1964, p. 168.

43. Frank Finch. "Fans to Honor Snider During Fete Twin Bill." *The Los Angeles Times*. August 26, 1960, p. C2.

44. John Holway. *Voices from the Great Black Baseball Leagues*. (New York: Dodd, Mead & Co.) 1975, p. 327.

45. "Elites Win Over Stars, Monarchs." *The Chicago Defender*. July 20, 1946, p.10.

46. "Revamped Elites Take 3 Straight to Head Eagles." *The Afro-American*. July 20, 1946, p. 18.

47. "Balto., Newark Locked in Tie for NNL Leadership." *The Afro-American*. July 27, 1946, p. 17.

48. "Cubans, Black Yanks Beat Elites, Stars." *The Chicago Defender*. August 17, 1946, p. 11.

49. Statistics sheet titled, "The Records of the Negro National League Are Final, and Are for Immediate Release." Art Carter Papers, Box 170-19. Folder 13. Manuscript Division, Moorland-Spingarn Research Center, Howard University.

50. "Relieved." *The Afro-American*. December 28, 1946, p. 12.

51. "Wilson May Resign As National League Head." *The Chicago Defender*. December 8, 1945, p. 9.

52. "Minister Elected Head of Negro National League." *The Chicago Defender*. January 11, 1947, p. 1.

53. Letter from Effa Manley to Cum Posey, January 12, 1946. Effa Manley, Newark Eagles Papers. Charles F. Cummings New Jersey Information Room. Newark Public Library. Newark, New Jersey.

54. "N.Y. Minister New NLL Prexy." *The Afro-American.* January 11, 1947, p. 19.

55. "Minister Elected Head of Negro National League," p. 1.

56. "Gray's Protest Over Kimbro Delays the Game." *The Afro-American.* September 7, 1940, p. 19.

57. "Minister Elected Head of Negro National League," p. 11.

58. "Memphis Gets 1938 American League Pennant." *The Chicago Defender.* December 17, 1938, p. 9.

59. Ibid.

60. Staff correspondent. "Owners Oust Tom Wilson, Install First 'Independent' Administration." *The Afro-American.* January 11, 1947, p. 19.

61. "Baltimore Gets Police Sergeant." *The Afro-American.* February 1, 1947, p. 8.

62. Dick Powell. "Wes Barrow Is New Manager For Baltimore." *The Chicago Defender.* February 8, 1947, p. 20

63. Ibid.

64. "Elites Win Two of Three From Stars in '47 Debut." *The Afro-American.* May 10, 1947, p. 17.

65. "Tom Wilson 'Strikes Out.'" *The Chicago Defender.* May 24, 1947, p. 20.

66. Frazier "Slow" Robinson with Paul Bauer. *Catching Dreams: My Life in the Negro Baseball Leagues.* (Syracuse, NY: Syracuse University Press) 1999, p. 117.

67. "Candy Jim Taylor to Pilot '48 Balto. Elites." *The Afro-American.* January 24, 1948, p. 17.

68. "Cleveland Signs Negro Second Baseman." *The Chicago Daily Tribune.* July 3, 1947, p. 21.

69. "Eagles Triumph, 10–9, 4–3." *The New York Times.* July 28, 1947, p. 19. "Cubans Halt Elites, 10–5." *The New York Times.* August 4, 1947, p. 24. "Cubans Strengthen Lead." *The Afro-American.* August 16, 1947, p. 13.

70. Testimony of Nashville attorney, Robert E. Lillard. Legal papers of Dallas Nicholas and William Gosnell. Vernon Green Estate. Thurgood Marshall Law Library. Baltimore, Maryland. Box 10A1a: 1940–1969. Proceedings from "In the Matter of the Estate of Vernon Green in the Orphans Court of Baltimore City." November 9, 1949, p. 61.

71. Ted Waters. "Numbers Found Lucrative Industry." *The Afro-American.* February 8, 1947, p. 7.

72. Clarence Brown interview. September 2, 2006.

73. "Mayor, Former City Solicitor Assail Rampant Prejudice." *The Afro-American.* January 10, 1948, p. 19.

74. "Letters Prove Not Enough to Change 'Onion' Stores. *The Afro-American.* January 10, 1948, p. 1.

75. "Rocket Shatters House." *The Afro-American.* January 10, 1948, pp. 1, 22.

76. "Residents of Mixed Areas Like Situation." *The Afro-American.* April 3, 1948, p. 1.

77. "In The Negro Leagues: Baltimoreans Remember." p. 28. Two pages of a longer article from Charlotte Harvey's scrapbook with no other identifying information. Charlotte is the widow of Elites pitcher Bill Harvey.

78. "Ex-Baltimore Elites Hurler Dead." *The Afro-American*. June 12, 1948, p. 10.

79. Riley. *Biographical Encyclopedia*, p. 764.

80. Statistics sheet, "The Records . . . Are Final . . . ." Art Carter Papers.

81. "Candy Jim Taylor to Pilot '48 Balto. Elites," p. 17.

82. From an ad in the Baltimore Elite Giants program for the second half of 1947.

83. "Candy Jim Taylor Absent, Kimbro Takes Over Drills." *The Afro-American*. April 3, 1948, p. 7.

84. "Veteran Manager Dies in Chicago Hospital at 64." *The Afro-American*. April 10, 1948, p. 8.

85. "Jesse Walker New Pilot of Baltimore Elite Giants." *The Afro-American*. April 17, 1948, p. 7.

86. "Elites Sign Young Tennessee Collegian." *The Afro-American*. April 10, 1948, p. 9.

87. "Elites Play Cubans in New York Debut." *The Afro-American*. May 22, 1948, p. 9.

88. Audrey Weaver. "Desk Notes." *The Afro-American*. May 8, 1948, p. 33.

89. "3-Hitter Wasted as Giants Again Bow to Eagles, 2–1." *The Afro-American*. May 8, 1948, p. 28.

90. "Johnson, NNL Prexy, Acts to Break Up Rowdyism." *The Afro-American*. June 5, 1948, p. 9.

91. "Elites Sweep Philly Stars Series for Half Game Edge." *The Afro-American*. July 10, 1948, p. 7.

92. Statistics sheet, "The Records . . . Are Final . . . ." Art Carter Papers.

93. "Pennant Race Evolves Into Tiff Between Elites, Grays." *The Afro-American*. September 11, 1948, p. 9.

94. Ibid.

95. Robinson and Bauer. *Catching Dreams*, p. 140.

96. "Eagles to Houston," *The Afro-American*. December 11, 1948, p. 7.

97. "Black Yankees and Grays Quit Negro League." *The Chicago Daily Tribune*. November 30, 1948, p. B2.

98. "Negro League Dissolved." *The New York Times*. December 1, 1948, p. 40.

99. Lillian Scott. "Effa Manley 'Hotter Than Horse Radish.'" *The Chicago Defender*. September 18, 1948, p. 17.

100. George F. Will. "Taking a Bat to Prejudice." *The Washington Post*. April 15, 2007, p. B7. Wills was quoting from Jonathan Eig's book, *Opening Day: The Story of Jackie Robinson's First Season*. (Waterville, ME: Thorndike Press) 2007.

101. Sam Lacy. "Baltimore Elites Promise Town NNL Flag Because Owner Played a Parlay." *The Afro-American*. August 28, 1948, p. 7.

102. Neil Lanctot. *Negro League Baseball: The Rise and Ruin of a Black Institution* (Philadelphia: University of Pennsylvania Press) 2004, p. 320.

103. "Cleveland Franchise Moved to Louisville." *The Chicago Defender.* February 18, 1949, p. 13.

104. "Leonard, Wright, Bankhead Taken." *The Afro-American.* February 19, 1949, p. 9.

105. Riley. *Biographical Encyclopedia*, p. 829.

106. "First to Crash Yank's Fold." *The Afro-American.* February 12, 1949, p. 9.

107. "Chandler Decides Negro Aces' Status." *The New York Times.* May 4, 1949, p. 16.

108. Joe Reichler (ed.). *The Baseball Encyclopedia.* (New York: Macmillan Co.) 1988, p. 1211.

109. Riley. *Biographical Encyclopedia*, p. 213.

110. "NNL Folds; New 10-Team Loop Organized by NAL." *The Afro-American.* December 11, 1948, p. 7.

111. "Pearson, Lockett, Kimbro Blasting Ball With Gusto." *The Afro-American.* April 16, 1949, p. 8.

112. "Titular Series to Open Friday in Elites' Park." *The Afro-American.* September 17, 1949, p. 15.

113. Sam Lacy. "Former Grays' Pilot Agrees to Accept Job as Coach." *The Afro-American.* January 29, 1949, p. 9.

114. "Len Pearson Inks Elites' Contract." *The Afro-American.* March 26, 1949, p. 7.

115. Dick Powell. "Pearson Goes to Baltimore." *The Afro-American.* February 26, 1949, p. 8.

116. "Hoss Walker Elite Pilot." *The Chicago Defender.* March 5, 1949, p. 15.

117. "Pearson, Lockett, Kimbro Blasting Ball With Gusto," p. 8.

118. "Baltimoreans Take NAL Lead With Sabbath Wins." *The Afro-American.* May 14, 1949, p. 7.

119. "Elites' Streak Reaches 8 After 3 Over Quakers." *The Afro-American.* May 21, 1949, p. 7.

120. Riley. *Biographical Encyclopedia*, p. 335.

121. "In The Negro Leagues: Baltimoreans Remember," p. 28. Part of a longer article from Charlotte Harvey's scrapbook with no other identifying information. Charlotte is the widow of Elites pitcher Bill Harvey.

122. "Baltimore Defeats Chicago Elites in 2 Games, 5–4 and 5–4." *The Chicago Daily Defender.* June 13, 1949, p. C1.

123. "Baltimore Closes on Eastern Pace-Setters." *The Afro-American.* June 25, 1949, Section 2, p. 3.

124. "Elites Clinch Eastern Division NAL Crown." *The Afro-American.* July 9, 1949, Section 2, p. 3.

125. "20-Year-Old Wins First Elite Start." *The Afro-American.* July 16, 1949, Section 2, p. 3.

126. Edward Prell. "Eastern Negro Stars Defeat West Team, 4–0." *The Chicago Daily Tribune.* August 15, 1949, p. B1.

127. "Elite Giants Win Eastern Crown." *The Afro-American*. September 10, 1949, p. 15.

128. "Titular Series to Open Friday in Elites' Park." *The Afro-American*. September 17, 1949.

129. "Chicago Beaten, 9–1, 5–4, in First 2 Title Contests." *The Afro-American*. September 24, 1949, p. 17.

130. Baltimore Municipal Court Tax Records. Liber MLP 7174. Page 69.

131. Robert V. Leffler, Jr. "Boom and Bust: The Elite Giants and Black Baseball in Baltimore, 1936–1951." *Maryland Historical Magazine*. Vol. 87. No. 2. Summer 1992, p. 181.

132. "Elites Win NAL Crown." *The Afro-American*. October 1, 1949, p. 15.

133. "Elites Take NAL Title In Four Straight." *The Chicago Defender*. October 1, 1949, p. 15.

134. "Hoss Walker Fined for Brush With Umpire." *The Chicago Defender*. October 1, 1949, p. 15.

135. Clinton "Butch" McCord interview. May 5, 2006.

136. "10 States Enact Anti-Bias Laws." *The Afro-American*. September 17, 1949, p. 7.

137. "Catlin Passes MD Plumbing Exam." *The Afro-American*. December 3, 1949, pp. 1, 2.

138. Leffler. "Boom and Bust," p. 183.

139. Second page of a letter, circa 1947, from Vernon Green to Richard Powell. Courtesy of Barbara Powell Golden.

140. Leffler, *The History of Black Baseball in Baltimore*, pp. 110–113.

141. Letter from Richard Powell to Paul Fagan, president, San Francisco Baseball Club, March 18, 1952. Courtesy of Barbara Powell Golden.

142. Lanctot. *Negro League Baseball*, p. 355.

143. Sam Lacy. "Balto. Elites Report $18,000 Deficit, May Have to Fold Up." *The Afro-American*. August 19, 1950.

144. Ronald A. Rooks interview. October 3, 2006. Mr. Rooks, an appraiser of art and antiques, is a Baltimore native and attended several games at Westport Stadium.

145. Leffler. "Boom and Bust," pp. 182–183.

146. Minutes of Special Committee—RE: Elite Giants. March, 1951. Prepared by Joseph L. King. Courtesy of Barbara Powell Gordon.

147. Ibid.

148. Lanctot. *Negro League Baseball*, p. 374.

149. "Lennie Pearson to Manage Elites." *The Afro-American*. March 25, 1950, p. 9.

150. "Junior Gilliam, Roy Ferrell Sold to Cubs' Farm Club." *The Afro-American*. February 25, 1950, p. 17.

151. "Meet Junior Gilliam!" p. 57.

152. Letter from John T. Sheehan to Richard Powell.

153. Letter from Jim Gilliam to Richard Powell.

154. Letter from Richard Powell to Leroy Ferrell.

155. Letters from Richard Powell to members of Elmira (New York) Baseball Club.

156. Leffler. "Boom and Bust," p. 182.

157. "Cubans Trounce Elite Giants in Double-Header." *The Chicago Defender*. May 20, 1950, p. 19.

158. "Negro Elites to Play Baltimore 2 Games Today." *Chicago Daily Tribune*. June 11, 1950, p. A-2. "Negro Elites Divide With Baltimore Foes." *Chicago Daily Tribune*. June 12, 1950, p. E-2.

159. "Baltimore Wins From Buckeyes." *The Chicago Defender*. June 24, 1950, p. 16.

160. Clark and Lester. *The Negro Leagues Book*, p. 163.

161. "Rookie Infielder's Double in 9th Decides Opener at Westport Park." *The Afro-American*. July 8, 1950, p. 16.

162. "Pearson's Homer Gives Black 2-Hit Victory in Opener." *The Afro-American*. July 15, 1950, p. 17.

163. Clark and Lester. *The Negro Leagues Book,* p. 163.

164. "Clowns Bidding for Laurels in East Division." *The Chicago Defender*. September 9, 1950, p. 18.

165. "NAL Meet Set Jan. 4–5 In Chicago." *The Afro-American*. December 23, 1950, p. 16. "NAL Drops 2 Teams, to Operate with 8; Martin Sells Chicago." *The Afro-American*. January 13, 1951, p. 17.

166. Riley. *Biographical Encyclopedia*, p. 224.

167. "NAL Batting and Pitching." *The Afro-American*. July 1, 1950, p. 17.

168. James H. Bready. *Baseball in Baltimore*. (Baltimore: Johns Hopkins University Press) 1998, p. 182.

169. "Ban 4 Elites After Strike." *The Afro-American*. September 9, 1950, p. 17.

170. Hubert Simmons interview. December 19, 2006.

171. "Negro League to Open 44th Season Sunday: 10 Clubs to Compete." *The Chicago Defender*. April 28, 1949, p. B5.

172. Sam Lacy. "Sonny Wills Slated for Dodger Farm Club." *The Afro-American*. March 3, 1951, p. 16.

173. "East-West Game Set For Aug. 20." *The Chicago Defender*. June 17, 1950, p. 16.

174. "Fay Says." *The Chicago Defender*. July 29, 1950, p. 17.

175. "Monarchs Win 2 Games From Chicago Elites." *The Chicago Defender*. July 22, 1950, p. 16.

176. *http://www.minorleaguebaseball.com/news/article.jsp?ymd=20060225&content_id=43565&vkey=news_milb&fext=.jsp*. Accessed July 31, 2007.

177. McCord interview. May 5, 2006.

178. "Possible Suit Over Ban on White Players." *The Chicago Defender*. August 19, 1950, p. 17.

179. Robert O. Peterson. *Only the Ball Was White.* (New York: Prentice Hall) 1970, p. 197.

180. Larry R. Gerlach. "Baseball's Other 'Great Experiment': Eddie Klep and the Integration of the Negro Leagues." *Journal of Sport History.* Fall, 1998, p. 461.

181. Scott Pitoniak. "Elite Giants' Fill-in Remembers the Day He Played With the Best." *The Rochester Democrat and Chronicle.* July 1, 1998, p. 3.

182. Letter from Edward C. Bush to Richard D. Powell. March 26, 1951.

183. Red Smith. "Gaylord, Gilliam, and Joe Black." *The New York Times.* September 7, 1979, p. A18.

184. Robinson and Bauer. *Catching Dreams,* p. 176.

185. Mark Kram. "It Seemed Like It Happened in Another Century." *Baltimore News American.* August 9, 1981, p. 3E.

186. Leffler. "Boom and Bust," p. 184.

187. "Elites Shift Club to Nashville." *The Afro-American.* May 5, 1951, p. 18.

188. "New Orleans Offers Elites More of Same." *The Chicago Defender.* May 26, 1951, p. 16.

189. "Memphis Beats Elites, Clowns Phila. Split." *The Chicago Defender.* May 26, 1951, p. 16.

190. "Elites Face Eagles In Nashville." *The Chicago Defender.* July 14, 1951.

191. Clark and Lester. *The Negro Leagues Book,* p. 163.

192. Letter from Fresco Thompson to Richard Powell. May 25, 1951.

193. Letter from Chicago Cubs to Richard Powell. April 25, 1952.

194. Letter from Mickey Shader to Richard Powell. March 21, 1952.

195. Barbara Powell Golden interview. October 3, 2006.

196. "Richard Powell Obituary." *Negro League Baseball Players Association. http://nlbpa.com/3feb2004.html.* Accessed January 4, 2006.

Epilogue

1. Larry Moffi and Jonathan Kronstadt. *Crossing the Line: Black Major Leaguers, 1947–1959.* (Iowa City: University of Iowa Press) 1994, pp. 109, 113.

2. Suzanne Ellery Greene Chapelle et al. *Maryland: A History of Its People.* (Baltimore: Johns Hopkins University Press) 1986, p. 287.

3. "Yankee Farmhand to Face Orioles." *The Afro-American.* September 4, 1951, p. 1. Interview with Frank Lynch. August 8, 2007.

4. Jackie Robinson and Charles Dexter. *Baseball Has Done It.* (Philadelphia: Lippincott) 1964, p. 167.

5. "Race Trend in Maryland Held Good." *The Washington Post and Times Herald.* May 28, 1954, p. C12.

6. Ibid.

7. NAACP Papers. Section II. Box A329. Folder 1. Manuscript Division. Library of Congress. Washington, DC.

8. Robert J. Brugger. *Maryland: A Middle Temperament, 1634–1980.* (Baltimore: Johns Hopkins University Press) 1988, p. 552.

9. NAACP Papers. Section II. Box A329. Folder 1.

10. "Hotels Keep Negro Ban." *The New York Times.* April 8, 1954, p. 28.

11. Untitled article in William L. Adams's hanging file at the Enoch Pratt Free Library. Quoted in *The Sun.* March 19, 1979.

12. *http://www.oldwestbury.edu/faculty_pages/watson/mitchellpapers.htm.* Accessed June 5, 2007.

13. *http://www.baltimorecitycouncil.com/history.htm.* Accessed June 5, 2007.

14. "Victorine Q. Adams: Civil Rights Leader, Humanitarian and Schoolteacher." *The Sun.* February 23, 2007.

15. Ric Roberts. "Vic Harris Says Build Own Baseball Leagues." *The Afro-American.* August 8, 1948, p. 25.

16. Clinton "Butch" McCord interview. October 18, 2006.

17. "Effa Manley 'Hotter Than Horse Radish.'" *The Chicago Defender.* September 18, 1948, p. 11.

18. Jules Tygiel. *Baseball's Great Experiment: Jackie Robinson and His Legacy.* (Cary, NC: Oxford University Press) 1983, p. 157.

19. "Baltimoreans Go 'Baseball Crazy.'" *The Afro-American.* October 8, 1949, p. 1.

20. Larry Taft. "Climbing Mountain." *The Tennessean.* April 30, 1995. No page number.

21. "A Rich Base for Negro League Lore." *The Tennessean.* June 13, 1996. No page number.

22. James "Red" Moore interview. January 19, 2006.

23. Glauber. "Elite Giants: The pride," p. C12.

24. Mark Kram. "It Seemed Like It Happened in Another Century." *Baltimore News American.* August 9, 1981, p. 2E.

25. Article in *The Tennessean.* June 13, 1966.

26. Randy Weller. "Old Timers Honoring McCord." *The Nashville Banner.* February 15, 1996.

27. Joe Black. *Ain't Nobody Better Than You: An Autobiography of Joe Black* (Scottsdale, AZ: Ironwood Lithographers) 1982, p. 65.

28. Red Smith. "Joseph Black's Self-Diagnosis Proved Sound." *Winnipeg Free Press.* December 26, 1952, p. 14.

29. "Do You Remember Biz Mackey?" *Negro Digest.* February 1954, p. 36.

30. Eagles' Pay Scales. Effa Manley, Newark Eagles Papers. Charles F. Cummings New Jersey Information Room. Newark Public Library. Newark, New Jersey.

31. "Gilliam Gets '54 Pay Boost." *The Pittsburgh Courier.* February 21, 1954, p. 12.

32. William C. Rhoden. *Forty Million Dollar Slaves*. (New York: Crown Publishers) 2006, p. 116.

33. Stanley Glenn interview. January 12, 2006.

34. Hubert Simmons interview. December 19, 2006.

35. Mike Preston. "Little Leaguers Get Big Inspiration from Negro Leaguers." *The Sun*. March 31, 1993, p. 3D.

36. Scott Lauber. "Young Ballplayers Step Up to the Plate—and History." *The News Journal*. April 8, 2006. *http://www.delawareonline.com/apps/pbcs.dll/article?AID =/20060408/SPORTS/604080318/-1/NEWS01*. Accessed June 23, 2006.

37. Kevin Seifert. "Anderson Says Injuries Won't Bench Him Tuesday." *The Washington Times*. July 6, 1997, p. 4.

Appendix A

1. Bill Glauber. "Powell's Records, Memory Are Key to Historic Past." *The Sun*. April 29, 1990, p. C13.

2. Mark Kram. "It Seemed Like It Happened in Another Century." *Baltimore News American*. August 9, 1981, p. 2E.

3. Buck Leonard with James A. Riley. *Buck Leonard: The Black Lou Gehrig*. (New York: Carroll & Graf) 1995, pp. 19–20.

4. Black baseball teams predate the Civil War. Most Negro league historians limit the term "Negro leagues" to those professional teams who played from 1920 to 1951 in the Eastern Colored League, the American Negro League, the Negro National League, and the Negro American League.

5. Jules Tygiel. *Past Time: Baseball as History*. (New York: Oxford University Press) 2001, p. 130.

6. James A. Riley. *The Biographical Encyclopedia of the Negro Baseball Leagues*. (New York: Carroll & Graf) 1994, p. 208.

7. Dick Clark and Larry Lester (eds.). *The Negro Leagues Book* (Cleveland: Society for American Baseball Research) 1994, p. 162.

8. "Spedden No Longer Black Sox Boss." *The Afro-American*. February 12, 1927, p. 14.

9. Bill Glauber. "Elite Giants: Great Players, Even Greater Personalities." *The Sun*. April 30, 1990, p. C6. It is unclear what year the sale to Rossiter took place. *Philadelphia Tribune* sportswriter Lloyd Thompson cited Rossiter as the owner in 1924 in his statement that, "the Sox's owner, George Rossiter, the Hanover Street steak vendor, has been voted the best vehicle in the league because whenever he went to trade he always took his colleagues for a ride." (Typed notes dated 1924 in the Cash-Thompson Collection. African-American Museum in Philadelphia. Box 1. Lloyd

Thompson. Notes on Hilldale Baseball.) "Crush" Holloway, an outfielder for the Black Sox from 1924–28 and 1931–33 did not name the team's owner, but he spoke of Rossiter and characterized him as authorized to spend considerable sums of money on behalf of the Black Sox in 1924. Holloway called Rossiter "a great man." It is easy to see why he felt that way. In April of 1924, Rossiter paid Holloway's expenses and those of seven other players, to travel from California, where they had completed a season in the California Winter League, to Baltimore to join the Black Sox. Rossiter paid the players twice what they had made in California (John Holway. *Voices from the Great Black Baseball Leagues* [New York: Dodd, Mead & Co.] 1975, pp. 66–67). On the other hand, several articles in *The Philadelphia Tribune* in 1926 portray Spedden as the current owner. The paper names Spedden as the owner in "Officers of Both Leagues Re-elected" (*The Philadelphia Tribune*, January 16, 1926, p. 10). In another article, Spedden is shown representing the Black Sox at an Eastern Colored League owners meeting in August of 1926 (notice in *The Philadelphia Tribune*, August 7, 1926, p. 10). Earlier, in a January article, Spedden appears with Rube Foster, NNL president and owner of the Chicago Elites, and Kansas City Monarchs owner, John Wilkinson, prior to their attending "a baseball conference" in Chicago (photo caption, *The Philadelphia Tribune*, January 9, 1926, p. 11). A review of the (Darby, PA) Hilldale Giants' accounting ledgers between the years 1923 and 1931 shows that Rossiter and Spedden worked together in 1923 and 1924. Payments of the Baltimore Black Sox's share of gate receipts for games between the Sox and the Giants at Hilldale went to Charles P. Spedden for 1923 and 1924 at the address for Rossiter's restaurant. Records for 1925–26 were not available (Cash-Thompson Collection).

Rossiter was in charge by 1927. He fired Spedden at the request of the other Eastern Colored League owners, who charged Spedden with failing to turn over to the league its share of the 1926 World Series receipts, $385. Spedden had been the ECL's financial representative for the series ("Spedden No Longer Black Sox Boss," *The Afro-American*, February 14, 1927, p. 14). Spedden returned to being a shipping clerk for the Albrecht Company, a publishing firm (*Baltimore City Directory*, 1928–1930).

10. Riley. *Biographical Encyclopedia*, p. 49.

11. *Baltimore City Directory*, 1929.

12. Brad Snyder. *Beyond the Shadow of the Senators: The Untold Story of the Homestead Grays and the Integration of Baseball.* (Chicago: Contemporary Books) 2003, p. 68.

13. "Rap Dixon Is Baltimore's New Manager." *The Chicago Defender.* July 21, 1934, p. 16. "Sox Boss Tells Why No More Games Were Played in Baltimore." *The Afro-American.* August 25, 1934, p. 17.

14. Riley. *Biographical Encyclopedia*, pp. 598, 223.

Robert W. Peterson's *Only the Ball Was White* (New York: Prentice Hall, 1970) offers a classic, well-written synthesis of library research and interviews with many stars from the Negro leagues. Other books of interviews with Negro league players are John B. Holway, *Voices from the Great Black Baseball Leagues,* (New York: Dodd, Mead, 1975); Brent Kelley, *Voices from the Negro Leagues: Conversations with 52 Baseball Standouts of the Period, 1924–1960* (Jefferson, NC: McFarland, 1997) and *The Negro Leagues Revisited: Conversations with 66 More Baseball Heroes* (Jefferson, NC: McFarland, 2000).

For biographical information on players see James A. Riley's mammoth *The Biographical Encyclopedia of the Negro Baseball Leagues* (New York: Carroll & Graf, 1994). For comprehensive statistics by team, season, and player see Dick Clarke and Larry Lester, *The Negro Leagues Book* (Cleveland: American Society for Baseball Research, 1994) and John B. Holway, *The Complete Book of Baseball's Negro Leagues: The Other Half of Baseball History* (Fern Park, FL: Hastings House, 2001). Accounts of many players' life stories are available, including Joe Black, *Ain't Nobody Better Than You* (Scottsdale, AZ: Ironwood Lithographs, 1983); Roy Campanella, *It's Good to Be Alive* (Boston: Little, Brown, 1959); Monte Irvin with James A. Riley, *Nice Guys Finish First: The Autobiography of Monte Irvin* (New York: Carroll & Graf, 1996); Buck Leonard with James A. Riley, *Buck Leonard: The Black Lou Gehrig* (New York: Carroll & Graf, 1995); Bob Luke, *Willie Wells: "El Diablo" of the Negro Leagues* (Austin: University of Texas Press, 2007); Leroy (Satchel) Paige, *Maybe I'll Pitch Forever: A Great Baseball Player Tells the Hilarious Story behind the Legend* (Lincoln: University of Nebraska Press, 1993); Murray Polner, *Branch Rickey: A Biography* (New York: Atheneum, 1982); and Jackie Robinson, *I Never Had It Made* (New York: Putnam, 1972).

For in-depth treatment of the history of the Negro leagues see Leslie A. Heaphy, *The Negro Leagues: 1869–1960* (Jefferson, NC: McFarland, 2002); Neil Lanctot, *Negro League Baseball: The Rise and Ruin of a Black Institution* (Philadelphia: University of Pennsylvania Press, 2004); Donn Rogosin, *Invisible Men: Life in Baseball's Negro Leagues* (New York: Atheneum, 1983); and Lawrence D. Hogan, *Shades of Glory: The Negro Leagues and the Story of African-American Baseball* (Washington, DC: National Geographic, 2006).

Brad Snyder's *Beyond the Shadow of the Senators: The Untold Story of the Homestead Grays and the Integration of Baseball* (Chicago: Contemporary Books, 2003) offers an insightful history of the Elites' nemesis, the Washington-Homestead Grays. Janet Bruce's *The Kansas City Monarchs: Champions of Black Baseball* (Lawrence: University Press of Kansas, 1987) gives the history of the team many consider to have been the best in the Negro leagues.

Information on Baltimore's African-American community during the Elites' tenure in the city can be found in Robert J. Brugger, *Maryland: A Middle Temperament, 1634–1980* (Baltimore: Johns Hopkins University Press, 1996); Suzanne Ellery Greene Chapelle, *Maryland: A History of Its People* (Baltimore: Johns Hopkins University Press, 1986); Elizabeth Fee et al., *The Baltimore Book: New Views of Local History* (Philadelphia: Temple University Press, 1991); Suzanne Ellery Greene, *An Illustrated History of Baltimore* (Woodland Hills, CA: Windsor Publications, 1980); Harold A. McDougall, *Black Baltimore: A New Theory of Community* (Philadelphia: Temple University Press, 1993); and Rosa Pryor-Trusty and Tonya Taliaferro, *African-American Entertainment in Baltimore* (Charleston, SC: Arcadia, 2003).

INDEX

Page numbers in **boldface** indicate illustrations.

ART CREDITS

The illustrations in this book, indicated below by page number, are printed by permission of the following: Barbara Powell Golden, 3-5, 7, 9, 10, 17, 23, 38, 40, 45, 46, 48, 51, 62 (both), 71, 73, 85, 88, 92, 123, 150; the Enoch Pratt Free Library, State Library Resource Center, Baltimore, 13, 19, 28-29, 79; Charlotte Harvey, 25, 111; and James H. Bready, 76. The illustrations on pages 41, 53, 74, 107, 113, 118, 119, and 141 are from the author's collection. The picture on page 33 was drawn for this book by Dave Almy.